played professionally, and I only wish I had met him sooner. He has his finger on the pulse of the game and has continued to advise me as I help my youth players understand the nuances of the game, the recruiting process and the politics behind crucial decisions. As someone who remembers her own college recruiting experience, it is an incredibly overwhelming time and difficult to navigate. I wish I had been armed with this information, as I would have felt much more confident and empowered throughout the process. When staring down the recruiting process, it can be difficult to know where to start, and easy to get caught up in the sales-pitch of prospective coaches. Steve covers every aspect of the process. He addresses the pros and cons while reflecting on his own personal experiences to give readers all the information they need to make an informed decision based on what is right for their family, athlete and unique circumstances.

Rachel Wood, former National Women's Soccer League player, and President of Summit Soccer Academy

The scenarios discussed in Win the College Soccer Recruiting Game *absolutely mirror my own personal experiences going through the recruiting experience with my two sons, and I wish there had been a guide like this to reference back then. If Steve Gans made mistakes in his sons' recruiting process, just imagine how tough it must be for most Americans to find the right path; and thus, this book is essential reading about an incredibly complicated process that requires help and assistance. Steve provides the compelling balance of personal experience and best practice advice, in a most useful guide to a most uncertain process.*

Robbie Mustoe, NBC Sports Soccer Analyst/Commentator, former Premier League player, and parent of two former college soccer players

---

A must-read for prospective soccer recruits trying to navigate the college selection process. Written from first-hand experience – as a former recruit himself, now as a parent and, crucially, a highly-respected leader in the sport – Gans provides advice that can help readers avoid bumps in the road that could have long-term consequences. There isn't a page in this book that doesn't provide a nugget or two of wisdom you can use when deciding your next step.

Frank Dell'Apa / The Boston Globe and New England Soccer Journal

---

This book is a fascinating insight into a highly competitive element of our sport's wider eco-system, and one that is very likely to help produce more players for the professional game in Europe as well as in North America. Steve is as knowledgeable and passionate about the game as he is well connected – all attributes that combine to make his book as valuable for parents as it is interesting for those working in the sport.

Paul Barber, Chief Executive and Deputy Chairman, Brighton Hove & Albion Premier League club

---

Steve Gans knows American youth soccer based on his own personal and professional experiences, including firsthand having seen his own two sons play as youths in competitive clubs advancing on to play at the collegiate level. His book is an incredibly thorough summary of the issues that ultimately impact how the collegiate soccer recruitment process operates, and the considerations which ultimately determine whether a player is offered a roster spot by the key decisionmakers—coaches and college administrators. The book combines key facts with Steve's own family anecdotes to help exemplify the issues and concerns that dedicated youth soccer players and their parents must think about if collegiate soccer is in their plans.

Paul Hattis MD, JD, MPH and parent of two former college soccer players

---

Steve Gans has written a valuable, first-hand account of college soccer recruiting. As someone who has studied NCAA recruiting and experienced it as a parent, I believe that Steve has covered many of its most important facets from the perspective of someone who has been through the process three times. Moreover, Steve provides advice in a concise, easy-to-read format that will help those interested in playing college soccer approach recruiting from a realistic perspective that emphasizes the player's well-being and love for the game.

Alfred C. Yen, Professor of Law and Dean's Distinguished Scholar, Boston College Law School and parent of a former college soccer player

---

College recruiting is very individualistic to everyone's own child so parents beware of the process to avoid the disappointment that may follow as a result of not being fully informed of the "how's and why's". Steve's personal experiences with his sons can offer insight to any parent or player, irrespective of sport, as they delve into the world of college athletics, the coach/player relationship and the admissions process. Finding a suitable college that matches the wants, needs and values of your student athlete will determine if it's the right fit! This book is a must read for the student-athlete.

Louise Waxler, Executive Director, McLean Youth Soccer

While Steve advised me during my pro playing career and afterwards, I only wish I knew him or had been armed with this knowledge to guide me and my family through my own earlier college recruitment process. The system is daunting from the perspective of an underprivileged family and its only now, after a career in football, that I understand the impact the education and college choices have had on my career outside of sport. The knowledge, experience and advice that Steve shares will definitely help any prospective athlete. Steve is very virtuous and sincere, and this book is written from the heart with first-hand experience to help families. It's a must read.

Paul Keegan, former Major League Soccer and Scottish Premiership player

Steve Gans and I met ten years ago on the sidelines of games as club soccer parents when our boys played together. Having been the beneficiary of his sage advice on a personal 1:1 level many times since then, I am pleased to see Steve's wisdom brought to a larger audience through his new book. The recruiting process can be opaque, frustrating, and stressful both for parents and players – Steve provides both expert guidance and also personal anecdotes that help highlight the human side of the process. The soccer element aside, college recruiting happens during formative years for the teenage kids going through it, and Steve helps the reader see the process through that multidimensional lens.

Chris Lemley, President, Sentry Auto Group, and parent of a current college soccer player

If you are the parent of a soccer playing college hopeful who is entering the college recruiting process, author Steve Gans feels your pain. In his book "Win the College Soccer Recruiting Game", he's taken the personal experiences of his two highly recruited sons, along with his years of experience and contacts as a soccer player, coach, parent and attorney, and written the how-to book you need right now. Every chapter includes practical advice, real world scenarios and useful insights to keep you and your athlete moving in the right direction. With limited scholarships, diminishing roster spots and ever increasing pressure on soccer coaches to win to keep their jobs, it may feel like your son or daughter is entering the recruiting Twilight Zone and you wouldn't be wrong. Steve thought he knew how the recruiting process worked, until he didn't. In the end he was able to help his sons have very positive college soccer experiences, but not at the schools they expected. As a parent Steve helped his sons negotiate the recruiting process and succeed. He can help your family, too. You now have an expert friend to guide you.

Lynn Berling-Manuel, Managing Director of the Women's Independent Soccer League (WISL), former CEO of United Soccer Coaches, former CEO & Publisher of Soccer America Communications

---

When I think back to my personal recruiting journey all those years ago, I remember not understanding how it all worked --- the evaluation/identification process, the rules, timetable and best ways to contact coaches. Oddly enough, all these years later most prospective student-athletes and parents STILL don't fully understand how it goes. Steve Gans has participated in virtually every segment of the American ecosystem, including of course the college recruiting process. His perspective and advice is invaluable for players, parents and even coaches who need to learn and understand the fundamentals, realities and best practices that lead to positive outcomes in the college recruiting process. A must read for parents and student-athletes looking to better understand the college recruiting landscape, and their personal roles and responsibilities.

Ted Priestly, founder of Fundraise4U.Net and former Division 1 Men's Soccer Head Coach

---

Steve Gans is singularly qualified – earned through his experience as a soccer parent, attorney, club soccer board member and player – to provide insight for athletes and their families into the college soccer recruiting process. This clearly-written guide blends useful, practical tips with sage, ethical advice. At its heart, this is an indispensable handbook based on Gans' deep understanding of the sport in this country and the desire of young players and their guidance teams to find the best possible academic and playing fit. Read it now, then keep it close by as a reference throughout the process.

Brad Feldman, play-by-play announcer and executive producer, New England Revolution

---

When I reflect on my own college soccer recruiting experience, I am keenly aware of how lucky I was to sidestep so many of the pitfalls that line the recruiting process. Quite frankly, I was flying blind. A resource like this would have been invaluable. Steve Gans draws on his experience and expertise in the sport to provide a thorough guide for any potential college player. Throughout his career, Gans has dedicated himself, often at personal sacrifice, to bettering all levels of the soccer landscape. This book continues that noble effort by looking to the next generation of college players and providing an indispensable resource for college recruits and their families.

Connor Tobin, Executive Director of the United Soccer League Players Association and former North American Soccer League and United Soccer League player

---

In his book Steve explains and illustrates the complicated process of college recruiting through the lens of a parent, sports lawyer and leader in the game. He shares his plethora of knowledge and experience which is invaluable to those looking to help their athlete(s) navigate the complicated business of recruiting. Steve was my representative when I

Win the College Soccer Recruiting Game

The Guide for Parents and Players

Steve Gans

ALINEA

Alinea Learning
Boston

ALINEA

Alinea Learning

Boston, Massachusetts

Published in the United States by Alinea Learning, an imprint and division of Alinea Knowledge, LLC, Boston.

Copyright © 2023 by Alinea Knowledge, LLC

All rights reserved. No part of this book may be reproduced in any manner without the express written consent of Alinea Learning. Reprint requests should be addressed to **info@alinealearning.com**.

Visit our website at **www.alinealearning.com**.

Library of Congress Cataloging-in-Publication Data is available on file.

Print book ISBN: 978-1-7358107-7-5

eBook ISBN: 978-1-7358107-8-2

Cover copyright © 2023 by Alinea Knowledge, LLC

Dedication

To Noah and Josh, who have with grace faced challenges on and off the field, and who have worked so hard to accomplish much on and off the field. I could not be prouder of the fine young men you are.

To John Borozzi, my best friend in the game since our time together with the Baltimore Blast in the 1980's, who has done so much in the sport from youth to pro, and whose perspectives and advice over the years have been invaluable.

To my father, Werner, who escaped Germany, and brought with him to America passion for the great sport of soccer, and instilled such passion for the game in me and Noah and Josh.

And to Lori, who has been there from the beginning.

Contents

Dedication xi
Preface xvii
About the Author xxiii
Introduction 1
   My Own Recruiting Story 1
   Noah's Recruiting Story 4
   Josh's Recruiting Story 12
   Lessons Learned 16
Get on the Radar of College Coaches 21
   Introductory Email 24
   Playing and Academic Resume 24
   Highlight Video 26
Create the Perfect Highlights Video 27
   Securing the Right Video Clips 27
   Producing the Video 29
   Length 32
   Sequence 33
Identification Camps: A Necessary Evil? 35

Choosing the Optimal Identification Camps 39

When to Begin Identification Camps 51

Showcases 57

MLS Next, ECNL or Bust? 63

MLS Next vs. High School 69

Coaches Moving/Fired: Unpredictability 77

The Fickle Draft Board 81

Playing Out of Position 87

   Bonus Advice 90

Picking the Right Club: College Recruiting Services 93

College Coaches in Your Club 97

The Vagaries of the Recruiting Journey 101

Avoid these Mistakes 105

Appendix: Insights from College Coaches 113

   Interview 1: Head Coach · Division 1 · Men's
   Northeast Conference 115

   Interview 2 · Head Coach · Division 3 · Men's
   NESCAC Conference (New England Small College
   Athletic Conference) 121

   Interview 3: Former Recruiting Coach · Division 1 ·
   Men's Ivy League and ACC (Atlantic Coast
   Conference) 125

   Interview 4: Head Coach · Division 3 · Women's
   UAA Conference (University Athletic Association
   Conference) 131

Interview 5: Head Coach · Division 1 · Men's Ivy League Conference 135

Interview 6: Head Coach · Division 1 · Women's Ivy League Conference 139

Interview 7: Head Coach · Division 1 · Men's Big Ten Conference 143

Epilogue 147

Preface

I deal with issues in the soccer world every day, from youth, to college, to the pros. Through my experiences investigating college soccer programs (at the university's request), advising parents on recruiting, representing college coaches in employment-related matters, parenting two college soccer recruited sons, serving on the Board of a U.S. Development Academy (now MLS Next) youth club, as well advising several youth clubs, leagues and related organizations as legal counsel, I think I have experienced it all regarding the college soccer recruiting process as it may affect a parent and/or an aspiring player.

And yet, despite all I know, both of my sons had hiccups in their recruiting experience – neither wound up at the school to which they originally committed. The fact that someone with my experience and expertise can still have surprising, and perhaps disappointing, outcomes, underscores just how fickle the college soccer recruiting process is.

This book contains much of the advice and content I provide parents and players who personally seek me out for advice each year at crucial stages of the recruiting process. It is my hope that I can pass along much of what I have learned over the years, so that you and your child will successfully navigate this uneven, imperfect process, and avoid the traps for the unwary that so often lead to let down. At a minimum, you will certainly come out of it with a better knowledge base, sense of the college soccer recruiting landscape and process, and useful tips that will provide a better chance at success.

Book Roadmap: Within this book I address and explore many key subject areas which are essential for you to best understand the college soccer recruiting process, and to be prepared for all that might come your and your child's way within the process. The following is a quick roadmap of the book, and I stress that you should read the Introduction as well as every chapter, because there are essential topics and valuable lessons and tips throughout:

Introduction: The recruiting experiences of my two sons and the valuable lessons/traps for the unwary learned from those experiences, including:

- The potential consequences of being played out of position in club soccer for an extended period of time.
- Is playing at the titular highest youth club level (MLS Next on the boys' side, and ECNL on the girls' side) always worth it?

- The ranking of recruits in order/priority by a college coaching staff at certain schools and its practical effect.
- What is a "Pre-Read", and its significance and place in the recruiting process.
- The importance of strong communication and seamlessness between the coaching staff, the Assistant Athletic Director who is the liaison with/to the admissions department, and admissions officers.
- The value/importance of a good interpersonal fit and connection with the coaching staff, even if the particular school is otherwise a dream school.
- Due diligence to do on the coaching staff, and several important questions to ask the Head Coach and/or Recruiting Coach.

Chapter 1: How to get the attention of Recruiting Coaches – how your child can get on the radar of college soccer programs in which they have interest.

Chapter 2: The importance of a playing highlights video -- and how to construct the video.

Chapter 3: The relative importance of recruiting Identification Camps – a necessary evil?

Chapter 4: How to evaluate/select Identification Camps – how to tell which camps might be valuable to your child's recruiting journey.

Chapter 5: When to attend Identification Camps – how soon?

Chapter 6: Showcase Tournaments -- how to evaluate those Showcases which may be (and which may not be) valuable to your child.

Chapter 7: Whether your child's goal should be MLS Next (boys) or ECNL (girls) – does the highest club level make sense in all cases?

Chapter 8: MLS Next vs. High School – the tradeoffs.

Chapter 9: What happens if a Recruiting Coach moves/leaves within your child's recruiting process – the practical implications.

Chapter 10: The "Draft Board" – how to interpret it, and how it could affect your child's recruiting experience.

Chapter 11: The potential impact of your child playing out of position for their club – and when it is/is not appropriate for you to speak up.

Chapter 12: Your club's recruiting services and resources – or lack thereof.

Chapter 13: College coaches in your club – pluses and minuses.

Chapter 14: A story which underscores the unpredictability of the recruiting process – thin margins.

Chapter 15: Mistakes I made as a dad within the recruiting process – told so you can avoid them.

Appendix: Hear from Head Coaches and Recruiting Coaches of college soccer programs themselves – what they look for in a player and where they look.

Epilogue

Disclaimer I: In order to best pass along guidance and traps for the unwary, I often refer herein to the specific recruiting experiences of my sons, Noah and Josh, and so it is important to note that the views expressed related to those experiences are mine, and not necessarily in all cases those of Noah and/or Josh, as the case may be.

Disclaimer II: The information contained herein is based on my personal experience. Although this publication is designed to provide accurate information regarding the subject matter covered, the publisher and the author assume no responsibility for errors, inaccuracies, omissions, or any other inconsistencies herein. This publication is meant as a source of valuable information for the reader, however, there is no guarantee regarding the results of your child's recruiting experience.

About the Author

Steve Gans has unmatched vast experience in American soccer. As the only American who has been a player, pro soccer front office executive, advisor/consultant to players, clubs, management and owners, and an attorney representing players, coaches, clubs, management, executives, owners, and colleges – from youth club soccer, to college, to the pros to World Cup – he has unmatched unique experience and perspective. He was named one of Soccer America magazine's Top Personalities of 2017, and he is commonly asked to comment on issues within the sport, including by the New York Times, the Sports Business Journal, the Washington Post, ESPN, The Athletic, Soccer America, the Boston Globe, Sports Illustrated, the BBC and the London Evening Standard.

With respect to the college soccer recruiting experience in particular, Steve has counseled many youth clubs, leagues and related organizations, sat on the Board of Directors of a U.S. Development Academy/MLS Next club for 5 ½ years, investigated a college soccer program at the request of a major university (in a matter involving recruiting), represented college coaches in employment-related matters, and advised countless parents and players regarding the youth club playing and college soccer recruiting process. In short, there is very little in the sport of soccer he has not experienced or navigated.

And yet, despite all of his experience in club and college soccer, neither of his recruited sons ultimately wound up at the school to which they had originally committed. If this could happen in the Gans family, it could happen to yours. Through the telling of personal stories and the provision of practical lessons and recommendations, this book is meant to as best as possible demystify the college soccer recruiting experience, and help you navigate the mercurial, imperfect process, providing tips for getting recruited and pointing out traps for the unwary which arise along the journey.

Steve is a partner at the leading Boston law firm Prince Lobel Tye LLP. He lives in Newton, MA with his wife Lori and Super Mutt rescue dog, Mila.

Introduction

My Own Recruiting Story

I have been fascinated with college soccer recruiting since 1978, when I was going through the college soccer recruiting "process" myself. It was a much different time, with no club soccer to speak of, and no college showcases. The college soccer landscape was much different than it is now, with the Big Ten only having one college program on the men's side – national powerhouse Indiana University – and the rest of the Big Ten schools having club soccer programs at best. Similarly, the schools of the Atlantic Coast Conference had not made true commitments to their respective soccer programs; it would be a few years yet before they offered playing scholarships across the board. To my recollection, the Ivy League remained the best conference in the country at that time.

I did not have any guidance in the college recruiting process. My father was an immigrant from Germany who could not advise on the subject – he knew of Harvard and that I wanted to play for Brown (the Ivy power at that time), but that basically exhausted his knowledge of schools. I had contact from some Boston-area college coaches who came to my high school games, but was fortunate that a prominent coach from that era, Hubert Vogelsinger, had taken me under his wing. Vogelsinger was the former head coach of Yale, and he had written the first American soccer instructional book of note, <u>The Challenge of Soccer</u>. He had become the head coach of the local pro team, the Boston Minutemen of the North American Soccer League[1], and was a very influential coach.

With the backing of Vogelsinger, my recruiting opportunities expanded significantly. He recommended me to coaches and provided a written recommendation for me to use as well.[2] As a result, I received a recruiting letter from Jerry Yeagley, head coach of the number one team in the nation, Indiana, and was admitted almost immediately after I applied. I would have likely played very little at that powerhouse. Vogelsinger recommended me to Cliff Stevenson, the head coach of my dream school, Brown, but Stevenson wasn't particularly interested

---

[1] Vogelsinger had left Boston after the 1976 NASL season to become first the head coach of Team Hawaii in 1977 and the San Diego Sockers in 1978 (each an NASL team), but we stayed in close contact and he kept up on my playing development.

[2] I can to this day recall a sentence from that recommendation (surely written by Hubert's talented wife, Lois, who was the brains behind Vogelsinger's books, soccer camps, and other business ventures), which seemed to be part compliment and part critique: "Steven has great stick-to-itiveness when his interest is aroused…"

in me. I was however recruited by Brown's conference rival Cornell, and so I wound up there.

While still a high school senior I had been given a great opportunity with the brand new North American Soccer League team in town, the New England Tea Men: a chance to periodically train with the first team, and a part-time job in the front office assisting the team's Public Relations Director, Vince Casey. And then something amazing: Casey made me the game Official Scorer and Statistician. Deciding on and awarding assists on goals in NASL games was, for a 17-year-old, very heady stuff.

The spring of my freshman year at Cornell coincided with the second season for the Tea Men, and I would have to take a 12-hour Greyhound bus ride home from Ithaca, NY (which included a 3-hour layover in Syracuse) to Boston nearly every Friday evening for the team's Saturday home games. The bus would leave Ithaca at 6:00 p.m. on Friday, and arrive outside of Boston at 6:00 a.m. on Saturday. I would work the game that afternoon or evening, sleep at my parent's house, and then take a bus back to Ithaca on Sunday (the return trip did not have as many stops and layovers, so it did not take 12 hours).

Near the end of the spring the Tea Men General Manager told me that if I wanted to keep the opportunity I had to transfer to a school near home, and so I did, to Brandeis University in Waltham, MA.[3]

---

[3] Following the next season the Tea Men moved from Boston to Jacksonville, Florida, but I was not going to transfer to a college in Jacksonville.

I didn't know much (actually anything) about NCAA transfer rules, but as I was making my decision about which school to choose, the Brandeis head coach, Mike Coven, told me that he thought I would not have to "redshirt" (sit-out) a season per applicable rules, and that I would be able to play for the school right away. The preseason couldn't have been going better on the field for me, but a week or so in I was gobsmacked by a letter from the Eastern College Athletic Conference, informing me that I did indeed have to sit out pursuant to applicable transfer competition rules. I was devastated.

The original recruiting and then transfer experience was filled with fortune and misfortune (and some missteps), but thematically, the one constant is that I went through a process about which I knew nothing, and would surely have avoided missteps if I had had more information and guidance. I have been fascinated by the recruiting process ever since.

Noah's Recruiting Story

The college soccer recruiting world had become quite different by the time my two sons came of age over the last few of years. As anyone reading this knows, the club soccer scene is dominant (and glutted), and there are many, many college showcases and identification camps from which to choose – the challenge is verifying which of them are actually worth much in terms of helping an aspiring player to be noticed by a college of his/her ambition.

As a parent, I love my two sons more than anything. As their coach for many years, however, I bent over backwards not to show favoritism to them, a cardinal rule of coaching a team on which one's child plays. And so, as a coach and soccer person (doing my best to separate from the love and resulting natural bias of a parent), I think I assess the playing abilities of my two sons accurately and without inflation.

That said, I believe that my older son Noah is a gifted soccer player, who possesses some playing qualities that are rare for an American player. I often say what separates American male players from European and South American players – cultures which are fully immersed in soccer -- is the "millimeter" and the "millisecond." The "millimeter" refers to the comparative tiny extra space between a player's foot and the ball he has just trapped. If the ball is consistently trapped a millimeter further away from the foot then that of his opponent over hundreds of touches during the course of the game, then in this sport of possession and attrition, the player and team will be the worse for it. The "millisecond" refers to that comparative tiny extra time period it takes for the player to see the play develop. Not recognizing opportunities quickly enough in a sport where space closes fast similarly puts a player and a team at a disadvantage. Played on and up to a 120-yard long and 80-yard-wide field, with 9 field teammates with whom to keep track within the flow, there is no more complex team sport in the world than soccer. The constant repetition and immersion by players in these other countries in general places our players behind regarding these important playing traits.

Noah started playing soccer when he was 3, and he took to it and loved it immediately. Though not a perfect player by any means, along with the requisite excellent technical playing and ball skills, Noah possesses some qualities that are rare for an American: namely, advanced field vision and calm and equanimity, especially in high pressure areas like the 18-yard box. High level coaches who have seen Noah have often referred to his play as "more European than American", a comment with which I proudly agree[4].

Noah played in the U.S. Development Academy (the "Development Academy or, the "DA")[5] for his club, the Boston Bolts. His high soccer IQ (allowing him to see several plays ahead as they develop) and passing and scoring ability makes Noah a born offensive center midfielder: a "10" in tactical soccer parlance. The fact that Noah does not have blazing foot speed (one of his playing imperfections) also reinforces that center midfield is his proper placement on the field.

Noah led his Development Academy team in goals and assists from the center mid position during his 8th grade year. But inexplicably, Noah was moved by

---

[4] When I say that Noah is "gifted", I don't mean to suggest some notion of "from the hand of God." I mean, rather, that (along with natural athletic coordination) he began playing at a very young age, and he has worked awfully hard at it, and through that work and desire has developed some unique playing qualities for an American player.

[5] The former elite youth club/player league and structure run by U.S. Soccer, which has now been replaced by MLS Next.

his coach to outside/wing midfield during much of his key recruiting years, 9th, 10th, and 11th grade. A classic wing midfielder jets down the wing and whips balls in for the striker and attacking midfielders. Noah did well out on the wing but did not/could not play that position in that classical style. Rather, he used guile and his skills and brain to beat players and create, as opposed to relying on pure foot speed.

I was concerned for sure when Noah was first played out of position on the wing, but my initial better instinct was to trust that the coach knew what he was doing in the best interests of the team (and, of course, to be a team player). But as time went on and Noah remained out of position, placed where he could not fully show his playing attributes, I became very concerned. Playing Noah on the wing was not helping the team or Noah. And the issue festered much longer than it might have precisely because I sat on the Board of Directors of the club, and I did not want to leverage my power or access in any way – I did not want to be one of "those" people. So, I waited and watched the issue play out.

Having sat back for all of sophomore and for the fall DA season of junior year, I finally made a coffee date with the club Director of Coaching (who at that time was still the head coach of Northeastern University and was therefore not at every Bolts DA teams' games). When I told the Director of Coaching (the "DOC") that Noah had been put out on the wing for most of the last 2 years, he put his head in hands, and said (among other things) that that was neither good for the team or Noah. That evening he instructed the team's coach to put Noah back at center mid, but as we were soon to find out, some significant damage had been done.

In February of Noah's junior year, we embarked on a driving trip down the coast to meet with the coaches at Brown, Princeton, Haverford, and Georgetown. The Philadelphia stop on the trip was supposed to include a visit with the University of Pennsylvania, but shortly before we left, the Penn head coach informed Noah that he would not be on the final list of his 6 recruits. That was an omen, as Penn had been the first Division 1 college to make official contact with Noah when it became permissible on September 1st of his junior year.

The first stop from our home outside of Boston was in Providence with the then Brown University head coach, Pat Laughlin. Noah had scored a very good goal against the Montreal Impact DA team in 10th grade at a game at which the Brown recruiting coach was present[6], and while NCAA rules prevented Brown from making contact until September 1 of junior year, we had heard from the Bolts DOC following that game that Brown had significant interest in Noah.

Anticipating the inevitable question, I sat in the meeting with Laughlin for the first few minutes, just so I could explain about Noah being played at wing mid, and provide assurance that he had been moved back to center mid. Laughlin led and said to Noah "You've been playing wing midfield." I jumped in and

---

[6] https://www.youtube.com/watch?v=g0BRmj7IQvI

made the explanation, but Laughlin repeated the same statement. Then he added: "We like you a lot at center mid, but we haven't seen you enough there. We don't like you as much at wing mid, and so we're not going to use one of our (recruiting) slots on you."

Thud. The negative consequences of having been played out of position during the key recruiting period suddenly hit home like a ton of bricks. All in, Noah was contacted by over 30 schools during the recruiting process. In some cases, he was the top recruit for the program at issue, but for more programs he was not the top choice, and this is significant, because at many schools coaching staffs provide university admission departments with a list of their recruits in order of priority, thereby improving a very desired recruit's chances at gaining admission. Being played at a position in club soccer that any decent college coach would recognize as not his college position had hurt Noah, and it felt like he was a player who had slid on draft day.

Noah ultimately committed to Harvard University, but he was the 7th and last recruit for the program that year. Though his grades and test scores put him above the academic index for Harvard recruited athletes, we were anxious as, this was after all Harvard, and because we knew that it would have been better had he been the first or second recruit on the list. Nevertheless, we had good assurances from the Harvard recruiting coach, and it was that program and school with which Noah proceeded.

And then an unthinkable event occurred. A mere few weeks before early admission decisions were to be announced, news broke of a scandal within the Harvard men's soccer program. It was reported that some of the Harvard men's soccer players were sharing amongst themselves a Google document that contained inappropriate comments regarding the Harvard women's soccer players. The Harvard administration responded by shutting the men's season down with two games left on the 2016 fall schedule.

Over the next week we tried to get in touch with the Harvard head assistant coach who had recruited Noah. The coach finally called back on the 8th day, apologizing that he had not earlier returned the call, but explaining that it had been a very trying and frenetic period. We were assured by the recruiting coach that no further punishment would be doled out to the soccer program by the Harvard administration. However, it soon became clear that the incident had transformed the men's soccer program from desirable to pariah status (at least for the short term) in the eyes of the administration and the Harvard admissions office. On the day of early admission (December 11, 2016), a player recruited ahead of Noah was rejected, and Noah's admission was deferred.

When a player commits to a D1 school the other D1 schools who recruited the player generally move on for that year, and so if things don't work out with the school to which the player committed, the player is in a type of limbo. Division 3 schools generally complete their recruiting process a bit later, but for a player who is tracking to D1, a D3 school seems to be a mismatch on the field (of course, it can very much be a match academically).

When the word got around about what had happened with Noah, the coach of one of the top prep school soccer programs in the country, the Berkshire School in western Massachusetts, contacted me in an effort to have Noah do a post graduate ("PG") year there. A Mexican youth national team player had just decommitted, and the Berkshire coach wanted Noah to fill his spot at the attacking center mid position. The coach's pitch was that after a PG year at Berkshire, Noah would have his pick of Ivy League schools at which to play.

As Noah did not need any academic or physical seasoning (a common reason why athletes do a PG year), this was a most unorthodox consideration for us, but in light of the Harvard debacle, I was for it. However, Noah just wanted to get on with it, and he pivoted after the Harvard disappointment and quickly committed to Brandeis University of the University Athletic Association ("UAA"). Academics is a top priority in our household, and as we viewed it, the Ivy League, New England Small College Athletic Conference (Williams, Amherst, Tufts, etc.) ("NESCAC") and the UAA (University of Chicago, Washington at St. Louis, Brandeis, etc.) were the best academic soccer conferences in the country, but as a D3 soccer program, I thought that Brandeis was not the right fit for Noah.

But it was of course Noah's decision to make, and he chose to go right to school, at Brandeis. Noah had a dream first-year in college, starting and helping Brandeis reach the Final Four, and he was named to three All-New England Best XI teams by the New England Soccer Journal magazine during his college playing career. Though it is my belief that Noah was more appropriately suited for an Ivy League school both on and off the field, circumstances intervened, and it was of course Noah's decision as to where he would matriculate and remain throughout his 4 years of college.

Josh's Recruiting Story

My younger son Josh is also an excellent soccer player, with high-level ball skills and a good soccer brain among his most attractive playing qualities. Josh is not quite as gifted a player or as athletic as Noah, so I am tremendously proud of him for how hard he has worked to achieve a long-held dream of becoming a college soccer player.

Also best as a center midfielder, Josh can play quite well out on the wing as well. Josh similarly played his club career with the Boston Bolts, and for its DA team at the U14 level. Josh was not consistently one of the first 12 selected players on the Bolts DA team, and so as I discuss in Chapter 7, the question arose whether the title and status of a DA player was worth it. Josh was only starting the DA rules minimum 25% of the time, and was otherwise not receiving substantial playing time. The advice I usually gave the parents of boys on Noah's DA team in that predicament who asked if the DA moniker was worth it (as discussed at length in Chapter 7), was that it was not if their son was not getting playing time.[7]

I decided that I could not give that advice if I did not live that advice. Josh left the DA, and it proved to be the right thing for him both personally and for his playing career. Josh thrived on the Bolts National Premier League team and in high school (which he got to play after leaving the DA). He scored 24 goals his senior year of high school, and was named League Most Valuable Player, All-New England and to The Boston Globe and The Boston Herald newspapers respective All-Scholastic teams. He had emerged from his older brother Noah's shadow and set his own successful path.

Josh had recruiting interest from three colleges which would fit our ideal academic criteria: Emory University and Brandeis University of the UAA, and Bates College of the NESCAC. It was a close decision for Josh between Emory and Brandeis, so close in fact, that on the day he had to decide Josh first picked Brandeis, but then changed his mind and chose Emory (he hadn't informed either coach by the time he changed his mind).

It was a hard choice between a school and a program Josh knew well in Brandeis, and one in Atlanta far

---

[7] I would tell the parents that as a Board member I didn't want them to leave the Club, but that I was a parent first, so I wanted to give honest and caring advice in the parent's and child's best interest.

away from home; but one which would continue to allow Josh to forge his own path away from Noah's shadow. My wife Lori and I were torn as well, but quite proud of Josh for choosing the path less travelled. I was also doubly proud of Josh, for he had received his recruiting offer from Emory out of an Emory summer Identification Camp, something which, as explained in Chapters 3, 4 and 5, is not an easy thing to achieve.

Right after Josh received the Emory offer, the Emory coach went to admissions to do an academic "pre-read" on Josh[8], and the coach reported that the pre-read came back positive, but with a binary mandate of slight improvement – namely, Josh had to raise his ACT score by one point to gain admission to the school. That was a clear and bright-line task, one which Josh promptly met by raising his ACT score by that point the next time he took the test.

With Noah's Harvard recruiting experience still fresh (and having painfully learned through it that things don't always go as expected in such process), we stayed in frequent touch with the Emory head coach, so as to ensure that everything was solid, and that we could not be headed for a similar devastating

---

[8] A "pre-read" is a standard step in the recruiting/admissions process once a coaching staff has decided that it wants to make the player one of its official recruits, wherein the admissions department signals whether a recruit is likely to gain admission based on his/her academic profile (with or without extra weight being provided to the player being deemed an official recruit at the school at issue).

surprise of the type which had occurred two years earlier. The coach assured me that the path was smooth now that Josh had met the mandate of the admissions department.

And then, unbelievably, as they say, lightning struck twice. Two days before Early Decision admissions in December of 2018, the head coach called to say that he had just come from admissions, and though Josh had raised his ACT score as required, admissions had apparently now (two days before the admissions date!!) raised its concern that Josh had not taken enough Advanced Placement courses, and as a result of that, it was unlikely that he would be admitted two days later.

Well, I can tell you that in addition to the emotion of shock and disappointment, I hit the roof with anger, as this matter obviously had not been handled correctly. I did have perspective though (even in the moment), and in this case I want to be clear that I did not place considerable blame on the head coach, who I adjudged to be upright and honest throughout the entire recruiting process. Rather, as the coach was young and new to the school and to the position, I quickly inferred based on my experience that this shocking result was more based on communication breakdowns between, variously, the coach, the athletic department (i.e., the Assistant Athletic Director who was the program's liaison to Admissions) and the admissions office (more on this in the next Section of this Introduction).

As for Josh, he had a devastating first day in the aftermath of the shocking news, but we quickly pivoted back to the Brandeis and Bates coaches, both of whom re-confirmed their interest in him. Josh chose Brandeis, applied Early Decision II there, and was accepted without incident.

Lessons Learned

At this point I am sure you are wondering about lessons learned from these two recruiting experiences which I can pass on, to help you best avoid the types of bumps in the road both of my sons experienced. I would be glad to share my thoughts in the hopes that it can help you.

I suppose the overriding lesson from Noah's Harvard recruiting experience is that so-called "Murphy's Law" can occur at the worst times. The fact that news of the fall 2016 Harvard men's soccer team scandal broke mere weeks before early admission decisions were announced simply comes down to stunning bad luck. That is not a lesson about the vagaries of college soccer recruiting in particular, but rather, that "stuff" happens in life, and sometimes at the worst possible time.

That said, there are yet perhaps a few particular impressions I could share from that experience which could be helpful. Since soccer is so much a part of your child's identity and background, it is essential that the school be a fit, the soccer program be a fit, and that there is a good fit with the coaching staff. I liked the Harvard assistant coach who recruited Noah, but I had reservations about the Harvard head coach at the time,[9] as in my opinion he seemed aloof in a concerning manner which reminded me of my own head coach at Cornell some 35 years before. But despite that lack of interpersonal connection, it was Harvard after all, so Noah and I kind of minimized the concern. But in fact, in my opinion the head coach's aloofness ultimately rose to the level of callousness, and it both harmed Noah's recruiting experience itself, but also the aftermath of the disappointment that came at early admissions time.

Thus, even if your child is lucky enough to be recruited by their dream school, still make sure that there is a real connection on a personal level with the coaching staff and that they feel that they can trust the coaches. It does not matter whether it's Division 1 or 3, the emotional and temporal demands of being a college athlete are enormous, and it is more than likely that the head soccer coach will be one of the (if not the single most) most prominent and overarching figures in your child's 4 years of college. If the "fit" and the connection between your child and the head coach is not a good one, it will likely significantly impact (negatively) your child's college experience.

Though I thought I knew about all the traps for the unwary in college soccer recruiting by the time my younger son Josh went through the experience in

---

[9] That head coach has since left the Harvard program; so to be clear, I am not referring to the current Harvard head coach, who was appointed in 2020.

2018, I found that in fact I did not. I learned a very important specific lesson from the Emory ordeal, which will hopefully help your child's recruiting path.

As said earlier in this Introduction, I put relatively little of the blame on the Emory head coach and placed most of it on the Athletic Department and the Admissions Department. Why? The Emory head coach was new to the school[10], and he simply had not had enough experience working with the Admissions Department, and thus, the lines of communication had not been properly developed and established, such that he fully understood the significance of the messaging coming from the Admissions Department. That's where the Athletic Department should have come in, and the Assistant Athletic Director who was the liaison to the Admissions Department should have been more involved so that the initial academic read messaging from Admissions could not have been misinterpreted in any manner.

After the head coach first went to Admissions in July for the early academic read on Josh, the feedback he relayed was merely the binary need for Josh to raise his ACT score by a point. But a reasonable inference must be that to the extent that Admissions had a concern about the number of AP classes, surely it messaged that concern in some manner at the time.

---

[10] He had been hired the year before as an assistant coach and was thrust into the role of interim head coach on the eve of the season, as the then current head coach took an Athletic Director position elsewhere. He brought Emory to the NCAA Tournament final eight that season, and off that debut, had been recently named official head coach.

It would be diabolical for the Admissions Department to hold off raising such a concern until merely two days before early admissions in December; and as angry as I was at the time, I still had to rationally conclude that there was no way that any such scenario had occurred. Rather, I logically concluded that there was a communications breakdown, and the new head coach's nascent relationship with the Admissions Department personnel had to explain this glaring error. That's where I believe the Assistant Athletic Director who was that department's liaison for the soccer program to admissions should have done a better job of ensuring that the dialogue and messaging between the coach and the admissions department was clear.

Don't get me wrong; I was plenty angry, just not so much at the coach, and more at the administration. I waited until we had quickly pivoted to Brandeis and everything was on track for Josh there (as I didn't want to look like I was looking for any relief), and then wrote to the Emory President, the Athletic Director and the Director of Admissions. I told them that we had already moved on to another school, but that they needed to look at their internal communication policies, so that this would not happen so late to another recruit. I heard back from the Athletic Director with an apology and statement of commitment to do better, but time will tell.

Here is the lesson from the Emory fiasco: when doing due diligence on the coach, look into how long he/she has been at the school. If a good number of years, then you can reasonably conclude that the bumps and grooves between the coach and the admissions people have been worked out and established (but still confirm such). Ask the coach specifically about the following: a) communication directly with Admissions, and the coach's confidence in that; b) how involved is the Assistant AD responsible for the soccer program who liaises with the Admissions Department; and c) whether a recruit who has ever received a positive initial read (i.e., the coach's understanding of such) has ultimately not been admitted (and if so, the circumstances of each such case).

I learned that lesson instantly when the Emory head coach contacted us with the shocking news a mere 2 days before Early Admissions; and so when we went back to the Brandeis head coach Gabe Margolis, the second question we asked (the first of course being whether he was still interested in Josh) was about Gabe's communication experience with the Admissions Department. Gabe quickly assured us that between his head coach and assistant coach positions, he had been at Brandeis for 13 years, and that his relationship with the Admissions Department was established and strong. He repeated that Josh's pre-read had been positive, and that in his experience there should be no problems come Early Admissions II time a few weeks later; and thankfully, that's the way it went.

-1-

Get on the Radar of College Coaches

As parents, we have all been there: At the first beginnings of the club soccer journey (when our kids may be as young as 9 or 10) we are encouraged by a charismatic and convincing DOC that "the Club" is the best path to gaining entrance to the college of choice, or even to a playing scholarship from the dream school. If you are reading this book, you know that the club soccer path is a long and winding one, with many ups and downs. One thing is clear, while in today's world playing club soccer may in most cases be necessary to be recruited, playing for the club alone won't guarantee that your child will be recruited.

Almost all youth soccer clubs play in "Showcases" but they have varying value. Some exploration of showcases is the subject of Chapter 6, but as a topline point, the likelihood that the recruiting coach of the school of your child's dreams will attend showcase events involving your club is a measure of several factors, including the reputation of the showcase and the practical reality of the college soccer program's travel budget. As to this last point, it is important to keep in mind that no college soccer coach has the resources of, for instance, John Calipari (University of Kentucky basketball coach), who, when hearing about a player of interest out of state can just take a chartered plane and show up to that player's high school game. Separate and apart from showcases, there is no guarantee that a recruiting coach from your dream school(s) will appear at your club's games with any frequency, if at all. Since as a practical matter virtually no coaches will appear at your child's Fall regular season games as a result of the fact that they are coaching their own college games, that limits possible appearances (other than tournaments and showcases) to their Spring scheduled games.

As soccer is a so-called "non-revenue" college sport[11], the recruiting resources of soccer programs are limited indeed. Given the modest recruiting travel budgets, recruiting coaches must pick and choose as to which tournaments, showcases, club games and

---

[11] In contrast with the revenue sports football and basketball that generate large sums of money for universities, which reward such programs with vast resources, including large coaching staffs and recruiting budgets, and enjoy an ample number of athletic scholarships.

Get on the Radar of College Coaches

players it can afford to travel to and see in person. There are a small percentage of youth soccer players who through their playing exploits, exposure and/or reputation land on the radar of a number of coaches at a relatively early stage and as a result are proactively recruited, but the vast majority of players who will end up becoming college soccer players have to engage in proactive efforts in order to attract the interest of their desired college(s). This is especially so given the modest recruiting budgets of college soccer programs as noted above.

Recommended proactive efforts to attract a program's attention involve a combination of a) writing to the coaches (the recruiting coach, as well as the head coach if his/her email is available (as it is not in all cases)) to initiate a dialogue and to get on the radar of the coaching staff; b) providing a playing and academic resume; and c) submitting a playing highlights video.

It is important that this effort is done in a comprehensive (including each of the three elements above) and professional manner, for the recruiting coach is deluged with emails and videos on a daily basis, and your child wants theirs to be noteworthy. Yet, for the same reason (as theirs ought not to be burdensome), their submissions should be concise -- that means emails and videos of an appropriately concise length – lest the coach becomes turned off and does not review all of your materials (potentially missing something you and your child deem to be important).

Introductory Email

Your child's introductory email should contain the following elements:

- A description of why they are interested in and enthusiastic about the school and the program.
- Their academic background, and why they would be a good candidate for admission to the college.
- A brief description of their playing background (including position(s) and club and school for whom they play) to catch the initial interest of the coach (a more in-depth description will be contained in the accompanying playing resume);
- Reference to the playing and academic resume attached to the email.
- Reference to the link to their highlight video (ideally to youtube.com) included in the email.
- Their contact information.
- An expression of thanks for taking the time to review the submitted materials, and a restatement of their interest in the school and the soccer program.

Playing and Academic Resume

Your child's playing and academic resume should contain the following elements:

- In the top area: a) their name; b) their current club; c) their age group; d) their date of birth; e) a picture (if possible, but not necessary); f) their height and weight; g) their contact information (email and phone number); and g) their

nationality and country of which they are a citizen.
- Their academic information should include: a) their high school; b) their graduation year/class; c) their grade point average (GPA); and d) their SAT and/or ACT score (if they do not have one yet, note that);
- Your child's playing information should include: a) their playing position(s); and b) a year-by-year (e.g., 2022-23) listing of:
    - Club(s) they have played for.
    - Team within such club(s).
    - High school they play for (if any).
    - Honors/significant playing accomplishments. These may include, for instance: a) participation in U.S. National Training Centers; b) selection for U.S. Club Soccer ID2 Camps; c) any international training opportunities (of some challenge and pedigree – not just something anyone can pay for); d) selections to college ID Camp All-Star teams; e) selection to any combine or showcase Best XI's or All-Star teams; and/or f) any individual regional or national player ranking (such as by Top Drawer Soccer).
    - Playing statistics (i.e., goals, assists, shutouts, etc.).
    - Significant (one that a college coach would recognize as such) team championships.

Highlight Video

Your child's playing highlight video is an essential component of their submission to college coaches, and the hope that they land on their list of possible prospects. How one ensures that valuable playing highlights are captured, and how one produces and organizes the video is the subject of the following chapter.

-2-

Create the Perfect Highlights Video

As noted in Chapter 1, in most cases a playing highlights video is an essential component in the effort to attract recruiting interest from college coaches. That said, there are a number of threshold questions to be addressed to ensure that your child constructs an attractive and effective highlight video.

Securing the Right Video Clips

The first and most important task to navigate in creating a strong highlights video is ensuring and securing game film of your child, and video that captures their best plays on the field. As my son Noah played throughout in the U.S. Development Academy, that was not a challenge for him, as by policy every game in the DA was videotaped. Thus, we had our choice of video, and were reasonably assured that many/most of his top plays would be captured (of course, though road games were filmed at the home of the opposing DA club, there was no guarantee that we would have access to such film, absent cooperation by club administrators or a friendly parent from that club). Since my younger son Josh left the DA after U14, securing good playing video was more of a challenge, as most of his games were not filmed, and many of those that were videotaped were not shot in a manner conducive to ensuring high enough quality to capture well the desirable plays.

When the club does not film the games, parents have to take the task into their own hands and either a) jointly fund the retention of a professional to tape the games with similarly situated team parents who also desire film; or b) hire that professional videography company themselves. Some of these video companies offer their services in small package deals at tournaments as well. That is a viable option, but I always advise parents to take a broader view of the task of securing comprehensive enough game film for their child, for what are the odds that you are going to get enough good film alone from 3 or so games that your child plays at in a one-off tournament?[12]

---

[12] While a subject for a different conversation, in my experience the odds that you will get film that shows your child's true playing style and qualities from 3 games at a showcase tournament in particular is lessened even more by presence in the tournament milieu itself; specifically, as

Create the Perfect Highlights Video

Since those odds are not high, I recommend resisting the hard marketing sell from video companies which contract with tournament organizers, unless it is part of a larger strategy to ensure that you get enough good playing film of your child (i.e., a series of games/tournaments that are filmed). You need enough of a sample set in order to sift through and find the right examples which show your child's true playing qualities. Thus, I do recommend that you have complete game film from at least 6 games (but ideally 10 or more or even the whole season (and some from preceding seasons)), so that you can sift through and find the diamonds, leaving much on the cutting room floor. Again, if your club does not provide the service of filming the team's games, you may have to fund that effort yourself; but one way or another it is a necessary effort for the recruiting process.

Producing the Video

Once you have enough (and the right) film, you can then get down to the process of producing the video. While there are companies out there which you can

---

a result of the pressure to be seen by the 40 coaches ringing the field, I have often seen teammates (and as a result teams) play completely out of normal character at showcases (e.g., a wingback who normally holds suddenly overlapping down the wing on nearly every play, in a seemingly frantic effort to be noticed by those coaches – thereby causing the outside midfielder to drop into the back position), and thus there is a good chance that you will be scratching your head about why your child is not able to play in their normal manner and/or spots on the field.

hire to provide each of the following services: a) film games; b) select the plays within the game film to feature in the highlights video; and c) produce the video itself, I recommend ideally that you not fully outsource all of the above items.

Specifically, I recommend that you at least make an attempt with your child to select the plays and sequences to include in the highlights video, and don't fully outsource that task if possible. While these college recruiting/videography companies may be "professional" there is no guarantee in each case that they really understand the sport of soccer, and what may be important to include (as they usually provide this service in many sports). You may indeed have a good sense of what plays are important, and in any event, given the multiple years competing in the sport, your child will surely have a good understanding of what plays they think should be included. In this regard, don't automatically assume that the professional company knows more than you in this area.

One fairly shocking example comes to mind in this regard: I once saw a college recruiting services company post a soccer recruiting example of its work on its website, and the video consisted of nothing more than literally three minutes of the featured player distributing short passes up the wing from his left back position; one after another after another. There was no variation at all – no cross-field passes, no through balls, no dribbling, no defending, no receiving of goalkeeper distribution or other passes – just the same short pass straight up the wing to a

Create the Perfect Highlights Video

midfielder, time after time. I am not sure how that company believed such a highlights package would be attractive to college coaches, but I am pretty certain that it did not catch the eye of many.

If you have captured/secured enough film and feel confident in your collective (with your child) ability to select the clips which should make it into the video, then given the personal computer technology available nowadays, there is no per se reason why you need to hire a company to produce your highlight video. My sons Noah and Josh were both able to complete the editing/sequencing of clips and production of the video itself by themselves.

In the event that you do decide to hire a professional company for any of the tasks involved in creating your video, the ideal would be that you find one that does know the sport. As said, we did not use one of these companies to create Noah and Josh's recruiting videos. However, in putting together a video of Noah's college playing highlights (the college provides tape of every game) I did retain a company to do the technical work of putting the video together after I had selected the clips I thought should be included. I worked with one of the owners of First Scout Productions (based in New Hampshire), Ben Chastney, and I was pleased with my experience. Ben has a soccer playing background that I thought was quite useful to the process, for though I knew which clips I wanted to use and in which sequence, he offered his opinion periodically as well (sometimes I agreed, and sometimes I did not). I thought it was a useful and productive process, and I was pleased with the video that was produced.

Length

In terms of the length of your video, my answer is that it depends. Given the sheer number of playing videos submitted to coaches, many recruiting advisors recommend that length be kept to no more than 3-4 minutes, lest the recruiting coach becomes bored and/or truncates the video early out of necessity. The theory behind that advice is that one can get all of his/her best highlights into a 3-4 minute span.

In my opinion, there is a case-by-case answer to this question. If your child believes they can get all the clips in which will demonstrate their playing qualities in 3-4 minutes, then that is indeed a proper length. If for instance one is a defender who generally holds their position (i.e., does not overlap much) and whose main qualities (and attractiveness) is winning 50/50 balls, balls in the air and/or destroying offense of the opposition, it may be enough to show the best examples of such plays in a concise manner. If your child is a more offensive player who covers ground all over the field (e.g., a box-to-box midfielder), then a longer video might be justified. Noah is an attacking center midfielder, and as we had many different clips of his important playing qualities – dribbling, playmaking and finishing ability, along with his field vision – his recruiting highlight video was rather lengthy, at 10 minutes and 13 seconds. But it was yet received well by coaches. Also an offensive player (like Noah), Josh's video was somewhat shorter at 8 minutes and 59 seconds. The choice of length is up to you, but keep in mind the above parameters, and only include a clip if you believe it is distinguishing. In any event, don't force it.

Sequence

Many professional video companies recommend that a highlight video groups a player's clips by the skill demonstrated – for instance, tackling, dribbling, passing, shooting, etc. Given that the making of the video is itself a laborious, time intensive effort (capturing the video, mining that game film for the proper clips, producing the video), I don't believe that the skills need to be grouped (especially if you are making your own video); and I would submit that ordering it in such a manner may present a type of sterile quality to the video.

The one exception I would make in this area is that I recommend that goals your child scores should be grouped together at the beginning of the highlight video. Here is the theory though behind the thought that you don't need to spend the extra (editing and otherwise) time going back and forth between games in an effort to group clips by particular skills: EVERY clip included will demonstrate your child's playing qualities (if a clip does not, don't include it), so it is fine to just let the clips run organically by the game from which it comes. For instance (other than goals), for Noah's video the clips are grouped by game (i.e., vs. Albertson, New England Revolution, New York Red Bulls, FC Westchester, etc.) and/or event order (i.e., DA Showcase), irrespective of which particular skills the clips from those game demonstrate.

Composing and producing the highlights video is an arduous enough task; don't put more burden on yourself than you need to.[13]

---

[13] Again, we were able to produce Noah's and Josh's recruiting videos using an application from a home computer, and as samples for you to see in terms of production and quality:

You can find Noah's recruiting video here:
https://www.youtube.com/watch?v=yU50gPRztfg

You can find Josh's recruiting video here:
https://www.youtube.com/watch?v=QeGY812VPZA

-3-

Identification Camps: A Necessary Evil?

I won't keep you in suspense: Just like the highlights video, attendance at some carefully selected college soccer Identification camps is generally a necessary part of the recruiting process. The next few chapters will discuss ID Camps in depth, and importantly, will outline the traps for the unwary.

It is first important to know that ALL ID Camps are money makers for college soccer coaches. In many cases college soccer coaching contracts involve a salary (often relatively modest) for the coach, and as well a provision allowing a coach to supplement his/her income through the revenue (or at least revenue sharing) generated by a school's ID Camp. Also, in the case of the private ID Camps not run by/in connection with a particular college(s), the main motivation is profit, and involves payments to the attending coaches.

That said, though money-making may be the main motivation behind the ID Camps, at many of these camps there can be a chance for your child to be "identified" on the path to recruitment. Your task is to sift through which ID Camps actually can provide that potential real opportunity, and which cannot/do not.

The majority of ID Camps are held in the summertime, but it is important to note that with their growth and proliferation, versions of them are also run in certain instances in the wintertime and the spring (on weekends and during school vacation periods). ID Camps are open and marketed to high school rising 9th graders (i.e., the summer following eighth grade) through 12th graders. Other than that age group span, there are generally no necessary qualifications to attend these camps. Thus, as long as one can pay the fee for the camp, they are welcome to attend.

Indeed, I have been to some ID camps with my sons, the attendees of which included club players, non-club high school players, and some players who did not seem to play organized soccer at all (it seems that the parents of these latter participants might have misinterpreted the purpose of the camp, thinking it was a summer activity camp, or it seemed to make sense for another reason). Given that backdrop, the competitive quality of these camps is often very uneven.

Identification Camps: A Necessary Evil?

And yet, given the college soccer landscape and practical realities, ID Camps are generally a necessary element of the recruiting effort. As college soccer program recruiting budgets are relatively limited, you can never be sure that the coaches from the college of your child's dreams will see them play enough (indeed, if at all). Thus, ID Camps can offer your child another (and in some cases the only) opportunity to be viewed by college coaches (and given the ability to pick the ID camp, hopefully the particular college coach(es) of their hopes).

That said, even if an ID Camp is legitimate in that it is sincere about finding recruits at the camp, as no program selects all of its recruits (most programs recruit about 6 players per year) from ID Camps, and given the vagaries of these camps (e.g., sheer numbers of players, uneven quality of play, games occurring on adjacent fields), it is not an easy task to earn a recruiting offer from an ID Camp. Despite those dilemmas, for the reasons stated, attendance at an ID Camp should be a serious consideration.

The question is precisely which ID Camp(s) to attend, and when to attend it/them.

-4-

Choosing the Optimal Identification Camps

ID camps have become an entrenched part of the college soccer process, and accordingly, the number and type of them have expanded. Here is a summary of the types of these camps as I see them, plus some commentary about the pluses and minuses of focusing on/attending them:

- **College Specific:** These ID Camps are run by a college program alone, and there are no other schools/coaches from other colleges at these camps. Obviously, your child should only attend such a narrowly focused ID Camp if they have a clear focus on the college at issue. The upside of attending a one-school ID Camp is that your child will be assured of being seen by each of the coaches in that particular program. The potential downside of attending a one college-only ID Camp is that it is an all eggs-in-one-basket approach, and if the coaches at that school are not interested in your child, some important energy will have been wasted (as noted below, ID Camps are particularly demanding and grueling, and thus they must be kept to a reasonable number, lest your child suffer injury and/or burnout).

- **Specific College Plus a Few:** A variant of the College Specific ID Camp described above is an ID Camp nominally run by one college program but with recruiting coaches from a few other complementary schools attending. In most cases the main school will not want a college with which it competes in the recruiting of players to be present; so the other schools invited to attend may be from a different division (e.g., the ID Camp is held by and at a Division 1 school, and a Division 3 college is invited), or based on their respective athletic and/or academic profiles, may generally focus on different student-athletes. Given those parameters and the likely contrast in program/school profiles, at most you might find one other school at such camp (other than the host college) in which your child has interest. Thus, in effect this type of ID Camp has the same upsides and downsides as the College Specific ID Camp: namely, the assurance that you will be seen by all coaches from your dream school, vs. the all-eggs-in-one-basket risk that if you do not inspire interest from those coaches, no other

When to Begin Identification Camps

schools/coaches of interest will put you on their radar.

- **The Amalgam:** These are ID Camps that bring together coaches from multiple colleges in one setting. On the low end, the Amalgam ID Camp may have coaches from 6 or so colleges attending, and on the higher end there could be as many as 12-15 schools in attendance. The upside on paper of an Amalgam ID Camp is that your child will not be putting all eggs in one basket, and in theory there will be a chance for multiple schools in which they have interest to observe their play in such setting. Of course, you must parse this, and confirm that amongst the attending schools at the particular ID camp there are a critical mass of those schools of interest to your child – and that of course is a case-by-case analysis, depending upon the structure and make-up of that camp. The potential downside of an Amalgam ID Camp is the risk that coaches from the school in which you have interest either won't see your child play enough during the camp, period, or won't see them at the right moments (a desired recruiting coach not seeing one's child's best plays is one of the Murphy's Laws of the college soccer recruiting process). In this regard, in contrast to the College Specific ID camp, even if the soccer program of a highly desired college attends the camp, because it will only be one coach from that program, you cannot be assured of receiving a thorough look from your dream school even at an Amalgam ID Camp of appropriate size.

- **The Bloated Amalgam:** The growth and business of college soccer ID Camps has increased so much in recent years such that some entrepreneurs have expanded the concept of these camps to a size which is marketed as the "ideal" opportunity for your child, but in my opinion is a trap for the unwary. I call these camps the Bloated Amalgam ID Camps, and there are several of them that bring coaches from 30 different colleges together to observe 300 aspiring college soccer players in one setting. There is even one Bloated Amalgam ID Camp that brings coaches from 50 different colleges to observe 500 players! The marketed upside of these types of camps is that your child will have the chance to be seen in one camp by many schools they may have on their list. – ("Be seen by 50 colleges!"). This is the opposite of the all-eggs-in-one basket dilemma, and on paper it sounds enticing. But not so fast. The reality is far more complicated. Think about it for a moment: if 50 coaches from 50 schools are collectively watching 500 players (or 30 coaches from 30 schools are watching 300 players for that matter), what are the odds that the coach from your child's dream school (even if present at the camp) will get a thorough look at them? They are of course not particularly high. And, given the size and number of players present, it's almost a guarantee that your child's best and most

When to Begin Identification Camps

memorable plays of that ID Camp will not be seen in the moment by the coach from the school of their dreams. Given that backdrop, I strongly recommend staying away from these extremely large ID Camps, as I believe the likely downsides outweigh any theoretical upside (which, for the reasons discussed, is unlikely to occur).

Here are some important tips and traps for the unwary to be mindful of:

- **Scheduling/Don't Overdo It:** While an ID camp (depending upon its structure) may last from 1 day to 2-3 days, ALL ID Camps are physically and mentally grueling, as players can be on the field and/or in sessions up to 8 or more hours per day. Thus, make sure that your child does not schedule too many of these camps within a summer, and that there is ample rest and recovery time between each camp. I have had to talk many a parent down from a presumptive schedule involving too many ID Camps (often scheduled back-to-back). If your child is overscheduled, it will backfire.

- **Which Coaches Matter:** Many college ID Camps will market heavily to you in an attempt to entice you to attend. Part of your due diligence is to investigate truth in advertising. Here is an important tip in this regard: in most college programs, the only coaches who matter when it comes to recruiting are the First Assistant Coach (who usually is the coach responsible for recruiting), and of course the Head Coach.

Second Assistant Coaches and Goalkeeper Coaches usually don't have much of a role or influence in the recruiting process (with the exception of course that the Goalkeeper Coach usually does have input in the process of the recruiting of goalkeepers).

Thus, even if you receive an ID Camp brochure or email which lists a college in which your child has interest in attending, you should perform further due diligence. If the coach/representative of the college slated to attend is not the Head Coach or Recruiting Coach (i.e., the First Assistant Coach), then performing at the camp would likely be futile.

A personal experience is instructive in this regard. It was pretty well known that, as academics is a very important value in our household, along with an excellent soccer program, top academic schools were front and center on Noah's list of desirable colleges. I was surprised then to one day receive a personalized email from an organizer of an amalgam camp, saying that he wanted to make sure that we had seen that "Yale" would be "at" this upcoming ID Camp.

As said at the beginning of this book and elsewhere, despite having a deep soccer background, I made my share of mistakes in connection with the recruiting process of my sons. But in this case, I did already know enough about which college coaches have influence over

When to Begin Identification Camps

recruiting decisions in a college soccer program. I wrote the ID Camp organizer back and said that I understood that Yale would be represented at the camp, but that I saw that neither the Head Coach nor the First Assistant Coach was going to be that representative. In fact, I went on, that representative was NOT EVEN going to be the Second Assistant Coach. He was going to be, rather, the young man who was responsible for operations in the soccer men's soccer program; in other words, someone who was not even part of the coaching staff! Given that fact, I concluded in my reply email, why would that make us interested in the ID Camp? I never received a response back.

It is clear that the organizers had been more interested in the sales benefits to be derived from the superficial appearance of an elite school at its ID Camp rather than actually offering players and their families true value. This kind of marketing loophole is a trap for the unwary. As an aside, I had this point confirmed sometime later when a coach from a different Ivy League school with whom I am friendly – then a Second Assistant Coach (and thus not one with recruiting influence to speak of) – told me that he had been offered a significant amount of money to coach for three days at another of the ID Camps run by the same organization. Sure enough, when I eventually received a recruiting brochure for that camp, that coach was listed first in the list of coaches who would be present! This, despite the fact that he was a Second Assistant Coach! It was of course all about being able to sell the dream of the school in the marketing, despite the fact that this coach's appearance was essentially meaningless to the possibility that an attending player would be recruited by that university.

- **Keeping it Real/Keeping it Honest:** So, if you start with the premise that money making is a significant component of ALL ID Camps, how do you distinguish/determine which camps are potentially worth the time, effort and expense, and which are not? Which are the ones that actually may provide your child with a chance to be recruited by a desirable school?

ID Camps develop reputations in several areas, including how "real" they are in actually providing meaningful recruiting opportunities for players. I thus advise that you seek input from other parents you may know (from your club or otherwise) whose kids have gone through/are going through the college soccer recruiting process, in order to hear about their experiences and perspectives in this area. Those perspectives and opinions can of course be subjective, but it is my experience that certain truisms about individual camps do indeed develop.

I advise many parents seeking college soccer recruiting advice every year, and my opinions about the respective ID Camps are a significant component of that advice. I developed decided opinions about the value (or lack thereof) of

When to Begin Identification Camps

specific ID Camps while going through my older son Noah's recruiting experience. And though on balance I believe my opinions were extremely accurate, there are exceptions to every depiction and rule (one is noted immediately below).

There is one very popular smaller Amalgam ID Camp which I observed and adjudged to be primarily a money-maker (MUCH) more than a place from which many good recruiting opportunities come. I thus affirmatively advised my sons Noah and Josh to rank it lower in their picking of the camps they wanted to attend (and they in fact never chose to attend that ID Camp). Separately, I once advised a Florida father of an IMG Academy club player who was not having any luck in his recruitment experience. The dad is a really nice person, and so I spent a lot of time with him, sharing all that I knew and my full perspective. The pressure was on by the summer before the son's high school senior year, and the dad's anxiety was palpable. I advised on many topics including ID Camps, and I recommended against attending that particular Amalgam ID Camp. The son attended that camp anyway, and wouldn't you know it, he got a late offer from a very good D1 school directly through his appearance at that camp. It was a perfect timing thing, as that program had a late recruiting opening. This underscores that there are exceptions to every rule, and that you should work hard in your due diligence, and read and talk to as many knowledgeable people as possible on the topic; and

- **The Recommended Mix:** So, along with my advice that you do extensive due diligence to make sure that the ID Camp your child is looking at is "real", and that your child does not participate in many of these physically and mentally demanding camps in a compressed period of time, my recommended approach as to the mix of selection is as follows:

    o **College Specific:** If your child has great interest in a particular school(s), surely sign-up for the College Specific ID Camp (and/or College Specific Plus a Few) of that college (to the extent that the soccer program does indeed run its own ID Camp). Again, this is the best opportunity for your child to ensure that they are seen (likely extensively) by the coaching staff of the desired college. One quick caveat in this regard is that if a College Specific ID Camp has more than, say, 75 players in it, that may be a tip-off that it has more of a money-making focus, than an actual aim to mine and recruit players for the program. As stated though, the risk of attending a College Specific ID Camp is that if it is not a mutual match, then your child will

When to Begin Identification Camps

> have just expended considerable energy with nothing to show for it.
>
> o **The Amalgam:** That "all-in-one-basket" risk of the College Specific ID Camp is precisely the reason why I recommend that your child complements their attendance at a college-specific camp with participation in an Amalgam ID Camp. Obviously, the Amalgam ID Camp you choose should have an attending coach (at least the Head Assistant Coach) from a college of great interest to your child; and hopefully there will be at least one other college in which your child has interest represented at the Amalgam ID Camp(s) they attend.

For the reasons stated above, I would not recommend that your child attends a Bloated Amalgam ID Camp.

Win the College Recruiting Game

-5-

When to Begin Identification Camps

Eligibility to attend ID Camps begins in the summer following 8th grade (i.e., the rising 9th grade summer). Because college soccer recruiting cycles for girls and boys often diverge, I will provide slightly alternative advice on this issue related to your daughter (on the one hand), and your son (on the other hand).

My strong IDEAL advice (in a perfect world) based on experience is that your child should not begin to participate in ID Camps as early as the summer following 8th grade, despite any temptation to do so.

On the boy's side, to the extent that there is an exception to that recommendation, it may be in the following limited scenario: if your son has a dream school, it may be worth doing one (and only one) 1-2 day ID Camp that summer following 8th grade at such school. That way, your son can get to know the school's coaching staff (and that staff may begin to take note of him), and he can also begin to get a sense of the demands of ID Camps so that he is prepared when he participates during the time(s) that they really count.

The girl's side is a lot more complicated. In recent history, girls have generally often committed to colleges earlier than boys. And despite the NCAA's recent evening of the rule regarding when Division 1 coaches may officially make contact with a player (women's and men's coaches now cannot make such proactive contact until June 15th following sophomore year), somehow, plenty of girls are still committing to colleges earlier, still in many cases as early as 9th grade.

Thus, it may be that your daughter will have to consider participating in more ID Camps in the summer following her eighth-grade year, despite the risk of burnout that I speak about below. This book is based on my experience and observations, and as I have two sons and no daughters, that experience as a parent at least is limited to going through the process on the boys' side. So as to this advice regarding the timing of ID Camp participation, I want to stress that CAVEAT.

I did reach out to leading Division 1 coaches on both the men's and women's side, and they confirmed some of the disparate empirical information.

When to Begin Identification Camps

Specifically, as discussed below, in a general sense coaches do not particularly focus on rising 9th grade boys at summer ID Camps, as they are mostly focused on constructing/assembling their next recruiting classes. However, because of the fact that girls still often do commit to colleges earlier than boys, there is indeed a higher proportion of attendees at girl's-side ID Camps who are rising 9th graders, and coaches on the women's side will indeed often focus on rising 9th grade girls for real.

With that as backdrop, I want to STRESS that if you are reading this chapter seeking advice regarding your daughter, please take the advice below as that developed mostly from my own experience on the boys' side only.

Thus, my topline advice is based on my personal experience and observation. First, the personal experience, and in effort to help you avoid mistakes and traps for the unwary, I will admit that ID Camps is an area wherein I as a father made a serious mistake. My older son Noah's recruiting was the first time I had been through this experience in the modern age, so despite my pedigree in the sport, I did not have a firm sense of what I was doing when it came to ID camps.

The marketing emails from the respective camps came aplenty during Noah's 8th grade school year and given how Noah was tracking in the Development Academy, as well as his desire to be a college soccer player, it seemed to make perfect sense that he begin his ID Camp experience as soon as he was eligible.

The first camp he did that post-8th grade summer was an ID Camp run by the then Yale Head Coach along with the Wesleyan Head Coach.

And the first inkling that maybe I had messed up in my guidance of Noah came the first night of that camp, when Noah called home in distress. He explained that he was a having a very difficult time physically keeping up with most of the players, who were bigger and stronger than him. And it hit me: Noah had just finished 8th grade, but he was competing at this camp with and against boys most of whom were 11th and 12th graders. Though Noah is built well and is strong for his age, there is no getting around the fact that the difference in physical development between an 8th grader and an 11th grader is significant.

I got off that phone call concerned and sad about the stress I heard in my son's voice, and mad at myself for not having researched ahead the fact that the ID Camp would be overwhelmingly filled with older kids who would put a mere rising 9thgrader at an intimidating disadvantage.

By the end of that week, though, Noah had found a way to adjust to this disadvantage well enough, and through his undeniable advanced skills, technical ability and soccer brain, had actually made the Yale-Wesleyan ID Camp all-star team. Foolishly, I thought that the problem was solved, and that because Noah had found a way to compete, it would help his confidence and game to have successfully competed against older kids. Noah next did the Dartmouth ID

When to Begin Identification Camps

Camp that summer and also made the all-star team there that week.

Though I thought my guidance had been validated by those empirical results, I could not have been more wrong. It was damaging for Noah to begin ID Camps so early, and he grew to dislike them and to burn out on them. So much so, that when the time that really matters for ID Camps arrived - rising 10th and 11th grade summers – Noah was less than enthusiastic about his participation in those camps.

My other experience/observation having now gone through the ID camp experience is that, while camp directors are happy to take your money if you are a mere rising 9th grader, the programs on the boys side won't give you a serious look until you are a rising 10th grader and/or rising 11th grader, as their focus is on the next recruiting class for which they are planning.[14] So, while they may take some note of a rising 9th grader who excels at the camp, the rising 10th and 11th graders will be the ones receiving the most attention from the men's coaching staff at that camp.

It is thus my strong recommendation that your son does not commence the ID Camp experience in their rising 9th grade year, but that, he does begin participation in the camps in the rising 10th grade summer, and certainly takes part in the rising 11th grade year. On the girls' side, depending on the

---

[14] Note that, as noted above, per NCAA rules, a D1 program cannot make official contact with a player until June 15th following sophomore high school year.

program and level of play to which your daughter aspires, you may have to consider starting those ID Camps earlier. But my admonition about care to avoid possible burnout remains, for both girls and boys.

-6-

Showcases

Showcases are of course another theoretical avenue towards gaining college recruiting exposure. Since opportunities to have coaches from your child's dream school attend their league games in most cases will be limited, showcases, and tournaments that have a showcase element to them, offer another opportunity to be "showcased" – again, theoretically.

Like so much in youth soccer, showcases are a trap for the unwary. The ease with which a showcase organizer can employ the word "showcase" for their competition is unrestrained, but of course, in the caveat emptor society in which we live, one must look beneath the topline to validate that the showcase at issue legitimately may provide your child with a meaningful recruiting opportunity.

The top showcases on the boys side are the MLS Next showcases, as coaches from nearly all Division 1 colleges and many Division 3 schools will attend them. Depending upon the club match-up at those showcases, you might find anywhere from 20 to 60 coaches sitting on the perimeter of the field at each MLS Next showcase game. On the girls' side, the analog top showcase is the Elite Clubs National League ("ECNL") showcase. At both of these showcases you can be assured that the coaches will be there; your child's challenge is to make sure that the coach of their dream schools chooses to attend at least one of their games during the multiple day event.

From there, one must conduct due diligence so as to ensure that the showcase at issue is indeed a series of games, competition or tournament worth participating in, for there is no magic to the word "showcase" (and no bar to or test of legitimacy for its use), so as always, the truth is in the details. The recommended due diligence includes (similar to an educated review of ID Camps as discussed in Chapter 4), which colleges will be attending, and then following (if a school of interest is among them), which coach(es) from that school (i.e., at least the Head Assistant Coach) will be present at the showcase.

If you have satisfied yourself that it is a showcase worth attending, depending upon the size of the showcase, your child will want to take one other proactive step. Specifically, after receiving the schedule of games for the showcase, your child should email the coach(es) from the college(s) in which they are interested, and inform the coach(es) of the following: a) the dates (i.e., days) of the games in which they will play at the showcase; b) the respective opponents; c) the time of each game; and d) the respective fields (field location and field number at the field complex at issue) on which each game will be played. This notification of the coach(es) presupposes that your child has already made the initial contact with the coach(es) and sent the background recruiting information discussed in Chapter 1. If your child has not done so, the contact email regarding the showcase should contain that background recruiting information as well.

There are surely other generally-recognized legitimate showcases underneath the top ones discussed above at which a good many coaches attend – for instance, the Girls Academy on the Girls side, and the ECNL on the boys' side, as well as the Disney Showcase for boys and girls. There are other flyaway showcase tournaments which are established, and which a fair number of coaches attend, such as (for example), the Jefferson Cup (in Richmond, Virginia).

However, both because the label "showcase" is used liberally by organizers of events from high to low, and because the recruiting travel budgets of college soccer programs are finite and limited (even at the top Division 1 programs, given the fact that college soccer is a non-revenue sport), you must responsibly perform that due diligence to ensure that the "showcase" being offered is a potentially worthy one for your child.

A personal experience is instructive in this regard. The ECNL has been a long-established leading league on the girls' side, and by now is also a respected league on the boys side. However, the ECNL only debuted its league on the boys' side in the 2017-18 season. It was my younger son Josh's junior year in high school, a pivotal year academically. Josh had left the DA a few years prior, and as described in the Introduction, it was the right decision for him. Josh had been playing in the NPL for his club team Boston Bolts, but now the club was joining the ECNL (and the team was to play in the ECNL), and the question was whether to play for the ECNL team; for, aside from allowing one to play high school soccer, many of the ECNL requirements (including extensive travel) were similar to those of the DA. In the cost-benefit calculus of whether it made sense for Josh to return to a DA-like existence, we had to weigh the impact that regional and national travel might have on his studies during this crucial high school junior year.

The ECNL is well-organized, and it knows how to market. In the rollout of the boys-side league, a number of regional and national showcases were announced (e.g., Philadelphia, San Diego, Florida). I knew enough to dig deeper, as my feeling was that that new league was not ramped up yet, and so I called a Head Assistant Coach (responsible for recruiting) I know well at an ACC school and asked him if he would be attending any of the ECNL showcases during that debut season. He told me that

Showcases

he would not be, as he did not have the budget for it. He said that he had committed that travel budget to other more established boys-side showcases, as the overall quality of the ECNL was at that time yet unclear.

My hunch confirmed, Josh did not play for the ECNL team during that ECNL debut 2017-18 year. It was the right call, as Josh had an excellent high school season and club playing year, and a highly successful academic year. This was clearly the right decision at the time, but I do want to stress both for the readers' and the ECNL's sake that the ECNL is now established on the boys side, such that, the ECNL showcases have become generally respected; and thus, pending the necessary due diligence outlined above and the particular circumstances affecting your son, it may very well be a showcase(s) worth attending on the boys side.[15]

---

[15] It goes without saying that ECNL showcases are leading showcases on the girls' side.

Win the College Recruiting Game

-7-

MLS Next, ECNL or Bust?

The presumptive highest level of play (and accordingly, most presumptive prestige) on the boys' side is MLS Next. On the girls' side, it is the ECNL.

The question is: from the best-chance-to-be-recruited perspective (and assuming that your child is selected by one of the teams) does playing at the perceived highest level make sense? The answer is that it depends.

There is no doubt that, in the aggregate at any one showcase event, the most impressive and most comprehensive list of coaches will attend MLS Next (and formerly the DA) showcases on the boys' side, and ECNL showcases on the girls side. It is also true that as the most prestigious leagues in youth soccer, having an MLS Next (boys) or ECNL (girls) team on your playing resume will -- at least initially -- stand out.

But even if your child is able to attain that elite club soccer level, be forewarned that just reaching that level has little beneficial meaning from a recruiting perspective if they do not receive adequate playing time on their team. For, obviously, a college coach is not going to recruit a player solely from a listing on a player resume; rather, they have to see the player actually play (via film and usually in person --- the Covid 19 pandemic example and exception notwithstanding) in order to pull the trigger on a recruiting offer. Put another way, being able to state in writing that you are on an MLS Next (boys) or ECNL (girls) team will be eye-catching and an initial distinguisher, but it will likely be meaningless if you are not receiving adequate playing time on the team at issue.

This sounds logical, but in my first experience in the DA with my son Noah, it was remarkable, and I was struck by how many parents of boys who were not receiving much playing time asked for my advice about whether the DA was "worth it." In any competitive club soccer team in any setting one can assume that there will always be some players/parents legitimately disappointed in that player's playing time. The math makes it so. On a roster of, say, 22 players, and depending upon how deep a coach goes into the bench, there will usually be anywhere from 5-8 players per game who will receive no to minimal playing time. In the DA, the rule was that every boy had to start (and only start) 25% of the games, and the way that played out, a boy who was not in the regular starting rotation was unlikely to play enough meaningful minutes.

More than a few of the dads on Noah's DA teams, frustrated by the fact that their sons were not playing much, asked me whether I would advise that their son stay on the team with the elevated DA status (which meant a lot to the boy's identity in each case), or move to another club which would provide the boy with more playing time. In each case, my answer was the same: "I am on the Board of the Club, so as a Board member I don't want you to leave. However, I am also a parent, and parent to parent, I would advise you to leave and join a club where your son will receive meaningful playing time." It really seemed like a no brainer to me, because the DA status alone was not in my opinion going to get the boy recruited to the school of his dreams. The only way that could happen is if the boy played meaningful minutes so that a college coach at a game or showcase could see him play (and so he would continue to develop as a player). Granted, playing at a non-DA club might mean that you cannot count on every college of your interest to be at your showcases; but again, how helpful would it be if all of your child's dream schools attended the DA showcase and even some of their league games, but they did not have meaningfully substantive playing opportunities? I would submit, not very helpful.

So I would advise you as a parent of a son or daughter, please do not get caught up in the mindset of (as the case may be) MLS Next or ECNL at all costs. If your child makes one of those teams, they will always have it on their resume, but if they are not playing enough and they are not happy, please leave and go to a club where they will play and be happy. Happiness is the most important consideration of course, but in addition, moving to a club where your child will play is also most likely to provide the best recruiting opportunities for them.

In my family's case, my older son Noah was a starter on his DA team, and he was indeed recruited by his dream school (though things ultimately went askew, as discussed in the Introduction). When it came to my younger son Josh, and it became clear that he was not in his DA team's top rotation, and was only starting the mandated 25% of games (and not getting meaningful minutes in others), I said to myself that I cannot give that advice if I don't live that advice. We had a family meeting about it (Josh, my wife and myself), and though a sobering decision, Josh decided to leave the DA.

It was the BEST move he could have made. He started on his new club team, and by getting to play high school ball, experienced fulfillment and confidence-building success that he could not have dreamed of in the DA; including setting school goal-scoring records, and being named League Most Valuable Player, all-New England, and to The Boston Globe and The Boston Herald newspaper All-Scholastic teams. This was Josh's best path to being recruited, and he ended up being recruited by the schools in which he was most interested.

MLS Next, ECNL or Bust?

Same family, but two different stories. Again, don't view your club choice as MLS Next, the ECNL or bust. There is no one monolithic answer that is right. Your child should choose the path (i.e., club and team) that is right for their particular situation.

Win the College Recruiting Game

-8-

MLS Next vs. High School

As the ECNL (in my opinion, wisely) allow girls to (both) play at the top club level AND still play for their high school, this chapter focuses on the presumptive restriction by MLS Next on the boys' side, which (with limited exceptions involving private school waivers) prevents a player from also playing for his high school. [16]

It is clear that the DA generally did and now MLS Next generally does present a better technical and

---

[16] There is some thought that Major League Soccer may be moving in the direction of slightly relaxing some of the high school rules, but the fact remains at this writing that the practical dilemma for the vast majority of MLS Next players is a full-on commitment to MLS Next at the expense of the experience of playing for one's high school.

training environment as well as better competition than does high school soccer. But that's not where the inquiry should end, especially in the U.S., for a host of player development and cultural reasons.

When I ran for U.S. Soccer president a few years ago I had many ideas about how to improve the sport in this country, and in particular as to player development and the DA, my plan was to liberalize (partially – not necessarily totally) the prohibition on high school play which the DA demanded. In this regard, I was interviewed about the DA in 2018[17], and I believe that some of my answers then do still explain well my view regarding the dynamic between MLS Next (then the DA) and high school:

"The ethos of the DA should change to one which focuses on ensuring that players who go through the system maintain their joy and passion for the game. The lack of joy for so many American youth players was an early and constant theme of mine during the campaign... The DA should of course be demanding, but it should not be as alienating, divisive and joy sapping as it is for so many young players.

My father came from Germany and passed on his passion for soccer to me, and I in turn passed it on to my two sons, Noah and Josh, who have been immersed in the sport their whole lives, as players and fans. Noah played in the DA for seven years, but my wife and I looked up prior to his U-18 senior high school year and realized that he was losing his passion for playing, and was generally miserable. The

---

[17] <u>Soccer America</u> magazine "Confidential", May 8, 2018.

dedication to the DA and its opportunity cost (no high school play, a somewhat less than normal social life) yet presented something most desirable: admission to the college of his choice.

Noah originally committed to a leading D1 college, and the admonition in our club (complete with examples) was that college coaches would not let one leave the DA or they would likely pull their commitment for a player who left the DA. We were thus left with a torturous conundrum. Noah had come so far and sacrificed so much to be in this position, and to risk it now would seem illogical. On the other hand, he was clearly miserable, and it was painful to see. Of course, the love of our son won out, and we jointly decided that Noah would leave the DA for his final season, for a chance to experience high school soccer and to get back that happiness. I haltingly called the recruiting coach with the news, and to his credit, he OK'd the move.

Noah thus played his last season for his high school and for a regular non-DA club in the spring, and by doing so, he got his joy for the game back. As a college first year he helped lead Brandeis (not the school to which he originally committed) to the Final Four and was named one of New England's top freshman players. He loves the sport again, and his playing future is relatively unlimited. But it would not have happened unless he had left the DA as he did....

You can't play this game at a high level if you are not a happy player. So "joy" -- far from being a soft term for pampered kids -- is an essential component to developing elite young players and ultimately national team players…

U.S. Soccer has to liberalize the restriction on high school play, so that it is a choice for all players at the outset. If it is not, it will lead to burnout and indeed in many cases, actual resentment of the sport. In its myopic view, U.S. Soccer over-discounted the significant fact that playing high school sports is a quintessential America experience, and denial of that experience has some important detrimental effects.

I think what is key is that every kid gets the choice, and is not automatically forced into the dilemma of the DA opportunity having attendant to it the substantial opportunity cost of no high school. Prior to entering 9th grade, I asked my son Noah if he wanted to stay in the DA or play for his high school. At the time, reasoning that the quality of play in the DA was superior, he immediately chose to stay in the DA, and said, "Why would I want to play high school?" I continued to check-in prior to every high school year, and Noah's answer prior to 10th grade was similar – DA all the way. But when I posed the question prior to his junior year, Noah said "Well, it would make no sense to leave, as I have come this far."

That answer was a distinction with a huge difference, and in hindsight, it represented Noah's tepid cry out that he was losing his passion in the DA for playing the sport. He was being recruited by many colleges, and so inherent in his answer was a pragmatism that he had gone through the process for so long with the goal (i.e., admission to a top college) in sight, such that it would be foolish to upset that process, irrespective of how wistful he was about missing the high school experience. But it is clear that over time he realized that he was paying a big cost and missing out on a quintessential high school experience: representing your school and playing with your close friends from your formative years. The experience of walking around your high school but not being recognized for what in many ways defines you and related to which you have dedicated countless hours to reach an elite level, is inherently alienating.

It may dawn on them early in their high school years or not until the end, but I believe that many youth players start to resent the DA once they realize the huge cost they must pay to be part of the program, and then thereby lose some joy for the sport.

To further illustrate U.S. Soccer's misread of this situation, I would cite a few more examples. Noah played senior year only for his high school, and the fear that somehow he would lose his technical edge by not playing in the DA for those three months went unrealized. Noah did not lose any technical sharpness or abilities, and indeed, I believe the less refined and more physical nature (athleticism over technical skills) of high school soccer actually enhanced his readiness to be a college player, as it rounded his game off.

Moreover, if U.S. Soccer's focus ... is to create players who are better prepared to be professionals, then I would submit that the high school game milieu does a better job in this regard then does the DA. To wit, the typical DA game (especially in the fall when there are few college coaches scouting) is attended by 40 white-knuckled (intense but simmering) parents and one USSF observer. The atmosphere is, to put it mildly, pretty sterile. Contrast that with many high school games which, at least in the game against the school rival, is apt to draw hundreds of fans or more.

Learning to play in front of a large crowd is a huge part of elite player development. Noah started as a freshman in the final four this year, and the moment was not too big for him. I would submit that having played in front of hundreds of fans in an electric atmosphere vs. a high school rival during senior year better prepared him to play in front of thousands of fans in the college final four than did the DA.

It is true that while some DA kids would choose to play high school soccer, others would choose to forego high school, but the point is that providing the choice could go a long way toward helping preserve enthusiasm for the sport. Liberalizing the high school playing restriction should be a top consideration of U.S. Soccer."

In summary, it is empirically correct that (in general) MLS Next provides the highest level of training and play. However, missing out on the high school experience (from a playing, social and classic American rite of passage perspective) can indeed have a negative effect on a young player's development and the all-important maintaining of enthusiasm for the sport (the "joy" I refer to above).

The takeaway is that your thinking should not be linear regarding MLS Next. You should look at your

MLS Next vs. High School

son holistically, and make a decision about what will best serve him in his development as a player and a person (and most importantly, what will make him most happy). Will it be an MLS Next club and no high school play, or will it be a non-Academy club mixed with high school competition? This is a crucial decision, and hopefully the above discussion will help you evaluate in the best interests of your child.

Win the College Recruiting Game

-9-

Coaches Moving/Fired: Unpredictability

At its best, the college soccer recruiting experience is a winding rather than a linear journey. A Head and/or Recruiting Coach's level of interest, communication skills, fickleness (discussed in Chapter 10) and/or job change can materially alter the path on which one believes they are. This chapter briefly addresses the not infrequent occurrence of coach departure from a program, and how one should be prepared for that.

Head coaches (and then often along with him/her, the entire coaching staff) get fired sometimes, and if that happens during the time your child is being recruited, it can have a major impact. The new coach and coaching regime may not have the same level of interest in your child, and if so, you may regrettably be back to square one with the school.

More commonly, coaches move-on on their own volition for another job. While that of course happens with head coaches occasionally, it more often happens with Assistant Coaches, who are of course ambitious and interested in getting to the next level; and to the extent that they receive a lateral offer from what they deem a more desirable institution, a higher salary, or even a Head Coach position, there is commonly more movement amongst Assistant Coaches who are in charge of recruiting, and if it is the coach with whom you have established a relationship at the school, it could create a major dilemma.

While this may sound like a theoretical issue to keep in your back pocket, my experience (both with respect to my sons' recruiting, and in connection with the recruiting experience of several parents whom I have advised) is that a sudden change in coaching staff in the middle of the recruiting process is (regrettably) a not uncommon occurrence. And while the coach recruiting your child may very well maintain their interest in them, the school that coach moves to may not be of much/any interest to your child. More importantly, the interest from the original college of your child's interest will perhaps be in jeopardy, as the new coach(es) may not share the same level of enthusiasm as to your child as the prior coach(es) maintained.

Coaches Moving/Fired: Unpredictability

This possible scenario is a real one, and it underscores both the vagaries of the recruiting process, and why you should never put all your eggs/focus in one basket. It is not anything your child can control, but is something for which they should be prepared. Preparation involves both a) (again) having alternative schools in the pipeline as desirable choices; and b) your child being ready to promptly contact the remaining coach who makes recruiting decisions or the new coach(es) (as the case may be) in order to get a candid answer about where they stand as to their recruiting status, and whether the departure of the former coach with whom they had direct contact will in any way negatively impact the understanding about their priority/place in the program's recruiting process.

Win the College Recruiting Game

-10-

The Fickle Draft Board

While you and your child go through the often-unpredictable recruiting process, it would be helpful to have some sense of what is going on behind the scenes on the other "side" (that is, with and amongst the coaches whom you hope will recruit your child).

While it may differ from college soccer program to program based on such things as the newness of the Head Coach, the number of graduating seniors, or just the traditional/regular approach at the school at issue, in general, it is a good rule of thumb that a college soccer program recruits about 6-7 players in each recruiting class. Often colleges initially give new Head Coaches an additional few recruiting slots in the first year or two of his/her coaching stint, so the coach may build and/or change the direction of the program. If there are many graduating players in a particular senior class, the coaching staff may be able to recruit an additional player or two in the incoming first year class. Conversely, if there are few players departing the program in a given year, the coaches may be provided fewer than 6 recruiting slots for that class.

Assuming for these purposes that the coaches have 6 recruiting slots to fill in a given class, the coaches may initially target their ideal players, from 1-6. But such list of top recruits may change often during the process, based on such things as:

- The perceived level of the player's interest in the program, as expressed by the player and/or as gauged by the coaches.
- Whether the player will be a realistic "get"/match for the program from a playing level perspective (that is, does the team or conference play at a high enough level such that the program is likely to be one to which the player would commit?).
- Whether the player will be a realistic match for the program from an academic perspective (that is, is the player's academic background [including grades and test scores] good enough to ultimately gain admission to the school?).
- A shifting view of interest in a player (in this regard, a recruiting coach may have high interest in a player, but if he sees him/her have a bad game or two at a showcase or otherwise, the coach's view of the player may change in a negative direction, and the player may drop down on the list, and may even drop off/out of the program's recruiting list/plans altogether).

The Fickle Draft Board

- A change in the mix of positions to be filled in that recruiting class (in this regard, the mix of positions – goalkeeper, defenders, midfielders and/or strikers – may change based on a variety of factors, including injuries to current players, players who decide to transfer, and players who decide to use a remaining year of playing eligibility to stay in the program for another year).

I call the list of top recruits that a coaching staff might create the "Draft Board", and it is my experience that the above factors often result in a very fluid recruiting list. Lack of timely communication from the coach with whom your child has contact can be attributed to poor communication skills, but it may also be indicative of jockeying of the Draft Board. So, your child should beware if a coach has been in consistent positive dialogue with them and then seemingly inexplicably goes "dark." That may be indicative of your child having fallen down on or even out of the program's recruiting list, either temporarily or for good.

A personal experience from my son Noah's recruiting odyssey may be instructive here. The first Division 1 college to email Noah on the first day that coaches were allowed to contact players (then September 1 of high school junior year; now June 15 following sophomore year) was Penn (the University of Pennsylvania). Others followed that day and more in the ensuing days, and that officially began the final uncertain leg in the recruiting process.

But dialogue with the then Yale recruiting coach[18] in my opinion evidences best this Draft Board phenomenon. Noah was in more consistent and direct dialogue with a few Ivy League schools other than Yale, and so it was somewhat of a surprise when the Yale recruiting coach wrote and asked Noah to come down to New Haven as soon as possible in early April of his junior year. Until then Noah had not had particularly "hot" dialogue with Yale, and so this somewhat emphatic and enthusiastic request was surprising. Indeed, the Yale coach asked Noah to come and visit as soon as possible one day during the next week (his message had come on a Thursday), and the coach specifically requested that Noah not wait until April school vacation a few weeks away.

An executive from a European soccer club I was representing at the time was coming in to spend Sunday to Wednesday of the next week with me in Boston, so as I planned to go on the Yale visit with Noah, he wrote back the next day (Friday), and asked the coach whether Thursday or Friday of the next week would work for a visit. The Assistant Coach did not write back that day, or over the weekend. No email was forthcoming on Monday either.

Noah wrote again to the coach on Tuesday reminding him of his request that Noah visit that week, and again asking if Thursday or Friday would work. And

---

[18] That Assistant Coach is no longer with the Yale program, and Yale currently has a different Assistant Coach who acts as the program's recruiting coach.

The Fickle Draft Board

with shocking bad form,[19] the coach did not write back at all!

My hindsight take on the matter: the out of the blue enthusiastic email urging that Noah come and take a campus visit as soon as possible that next week was motivated by the fact that a player Yale had in its top 6 on the Draft Board fell out of contention (either because the player said no or the coaches lost interest in him), which put Noah within the Draft Board. And then – perhaps in shorter than a day's time – Noah had fallen out of the Draft Board because another player in whom Yale had more preexisting interest became available.

Whatever the real story,[20] the moving Draft Board is real, and something related to which you should be aware. Again, a lack of timely correspondence from a recruiting coach with whom your child has had positive dialogue may be the result of nothing more than coach untimely/poor communication skills; but it also may be indicative of a material change having occurred in that program's Draft Board.

---

[19] Regrettably, such bad form from coaches within the recruiting process is not all that uncommon.

[20] We will never know the real story, but ironically, several weeks later the Yale recruiting coach wrote again, saying that the recruiting class was still open and asking that Noah come to New Haven, but not apologizing for having gone dark in the prior exchange of emails or referencing that correspondence at all. He got a piece of my mind in response.

Win the College Recruiting Game

-11-

Playing Out of Position

In a magazine interview about club soccer[21], I was once asked the question when it might be appropriate for a parent to bring their concerns about their child's experience to club leadership, and when they should bite their tongue, and I think my response then is a good lead-in to that question and related issues that could impact recruiting:

"Parents ought not to complain to coaches *simply* because -- absent something sinister behind the coach's decision -- their child is not receiving enough playing time in their opinion. When you think about it, it is a presupposition that about a third of the families on every team will be less than happy, because in a roster of 18-22 at least a third of the

---

[21] <u>Soccer</u> <u>America</u> magazine "Youth Soccer Insider", January 29,2019.

players will not be starting or receiving significant playing time. Given this inherent issue, the fact that you are paying tuition as a parent does not give you the right to complain or demand that your child should start.

I can think of a few examples where parent complaints to club leadership are absolutely appropriate. One I know about involves a situation wherein the coach had his (son) on the team, and he unabashedly favored that son in an effort to have him recruited by a high Division 1 school. That favoritism in and of itself broke the cardinal rule that when you coach your child you should bend over backwards to ensure that you *do not* favor him or her.

But also, in this case the coach's effort to showcase his (son) marginalized many of the other boys on the team, which had the effect of damaging the college recruiting experiences of a few of the boys. That was a situation for sure wherein parent complaints would have been appropriate."

I believe that as a general principle, absent substantial LEGITMATE concerns,[22] a parent should simply stand/sit on the sidelines, cheering on their child, but refraining from criticism or complaint. Your child not receiving enough playing time in and of itself is not the basis of complaint (though it may be the legitimate basis of reevaluation, and for guidance on that, please see footnote 21 immediately

---

[22] As mentioned in Chapter 7, the mere fact that your child might not be receiving adequate playing time might just mean that it would be prudent to move to another youth club where that playing time will be forthcoming.

below as well as the passage in Chapter 7 it references).

Similarly, as part of the lesson of youth sports should be the inculcation and virtue of teamwork and selflessness on the field, if a coach plays your child in a position other than their perceived ideal one in a belief that it is in the best interests of the team, you should grin and bear it – at least INITIALLY.

Because an important part of your child's club soccer objective is the pursuit of a successful pathway to college soccer (otherwise you would not be reading this book), however, – and while you SHOULD NOT overreact[23] -- I do think it would be important and acceptable to raise concerns in the event that your child is played in a position for an extended period of time other than that which they are likely to play in college.

As discussed in the Introduction, my older son Noah is a clear center of the park player, and the fact that he was played out on the wing for much of his key recruiting years ended up hurting some of his recruiting opportunities. Also as recounted in the Introduction, for various reasons (principle-based) I waited a long time before speaking with the Club DOC about the issue. In hindsight, waiting so long is one of my greatest regrets regarding the choices and mistakes I made during Noah's recruiting process.

---

[23] Both because it would be obnoxious and because your child playing out of their best position for a relatively limited stint in their club soccer career will likely not harm their recruiting trajectory.

So don't panic if your child is played out of position for a series of games. Don't be "that" parent – that noisy, obnoxious parent who attempts to intervene the moment something doesn't go your child's way. However, if your child is played at a materially different position than that which they are highly likely to play in college[24] for an extended period of time such that it may be hurting their recruiting, it might then be an appropriate time to speak with the DOC (or other coaching leadership, to the extent that you do not feel comfortable or familiar enough with the DOC).

Bonus Advice

While not specifically about recruiting, as every step along the path of the club soccer journey can impact where your child ends up in their soccer playing pursuits, I thought I would share a tip about when in another situation it may be ok to bring a grievance to the club DOC. Specifically, a question posed in a past interview with Soccer America magazine[25] (and my answer) might provide some guidance here, as follows:

---

[24] Either because recruiting coaches have told them the position where such coaches see them playing in college, or you truly understand the tactics of soccer to a significant degree (and it is important to note here as a reality check that at this writing there are still very few American soccer parents who actually fall into that category).

[25] Soccer America magazine "Youth Soccer Insider", January 29, 2019.

Playing Out of Position

"Question: I imagine that poor communication can lead to situations in which parents would have a grievance. Do you have an example of that?

Every year I advise many parents regarding college recruiting and during the time of tryouts for the next club season. One particular scenario I have seen often that is regrettably common amongst many clubs is the following: a player who has played several years for a club attends tryouts for the next season and does not thereafter receive any communication for a protracted period of time (though they know that other players are receiving offers for the team). Parents understandably become frustrated and perplexed, and they wonder what is going on.

In my experience, this sudden silence from the familiar club means that the player is on the "bubble" of making the team, and the coach is waiting out the process to see how many extended offers will be accepted. The awkward situation develops as a result of less-than-ideal DOC communication skills or policies, and simply put, long-serving club players and their families deserve more straightforward communication about where they stand.

That is a situation in my opinion wherein it is absolutely appropriate for a parent to contact the DOC to ask for a timely explanation."

Win the College Recruiting Game

-12-

Picking the Right Club: College Recruiting Services

No youth soccer club is perfect, but in my experience, some are surely better than others in terms of competency, and truly caring about the playing development and pathway of its players. That said (also in my experience), it is a basic truism that a parent who is provided an accurate primer on the merits/drawbacks of clubs on a relative basis as to such important measures as organization, commitment of the DOC and leading coaches to the players, and commitment to customer service, will yet in most cases be prepared to nullify/ignore such advice. Instead, they will likely make the overarching priority in any event the most prestigious club for their child (e.g., an MLS Next (boys) or ECNL (girls) club); as they believe it will be the surest path to college recruiting success.

Despite that reality, I wanted to give you some pointers on what to look for within a club which you may be considering or indeed already be with, in terms of its college recruiting services. While it is generally not a question one is primed to think of while coming in the door at say, U11, the college recruiting services and resources that a club provides certainly should be part of your due diligence process.

A club that holds only one college recruiting night per year could and should be doing more for its players and parents. In addition to holding in-person educational events regarding the recruiting process, a diligent club in this area should have helpful online college soccer recruiting resources on its website. Those resources should include substantive guidance and tips on the items I discuss in Chapters 1 and 2 – such as how to contact college coaches, what to include in your submission, the hows and whys of a recruiting video, etc.

Further, education and help in the college soccer recruiting process should be a part of the tuition that you pay to the club. When the time is appropriate in a player's development, a coach should help in and advise on the recruiting process – throughout the recruiting process -- and should be actively involved in such things as:

Picking the Right Club: College Recruiting Services

- Informing players on the team which college coaches may be scouting at the upcoming team game
- Being willing to contact college coaches on behalf of players on the team (though each player and parent should understand that the coach can only be expected to provide the college coach at issue with a candid assessment of whether he/she sees the player as qualified to play at the school at issue)
- Meeting with each parent and player to discuss the player's progress and the assessment of realistic college choices from a playing perspective
- Proactively showcasing each player as appropriate (i.e., playing the player in games at which coaches from schools they are interested in are present – and in the right position)

A club or coach which/who charges separately for help in the college recruiting process should set off red flags for you.

Win the College Recruiting Game

-13-

College Coaches in Your Club

Having current college coaches within your club (as team coaches or program directors) can be a very advantageous thing. Many of these coaches (as peers) have great connections with and ready access to coaches at other schools. Further, as part of their job is recruiting, they have first-hand experience in that area, and can therefore be a very helpful resource to you and/or your child during the process.

But I have also seen situations in which the coach has a conflict of interest and does not necessarily act in the best interests of the player. If the player is someone whom the coach would ideally like to successfully recruit for their own college program, will they really in all cases be helpful in recommending the player to another school in which the player has interest, say, a college in the same conference as the coach's? This scenario/possibility is a trap for the unwary.

In this regard, I know of a club player who came from an emerging country, and whose parents were not at all schooled on the intricacies of the recruiting process, so he received very little guidance from home. This player's dream was to play for a top 10 program nationally. His coach in the club was head coach of a good D1 program, but nothing approaching top 10 stature.

That coach seemed to do all he could to wrap up the commitment of the player as early as possible, and his energy was spent convincing the player to play for him in college. As a consequence, the player did not have any help within his youth club in terms of helping recommend or introduce the player to any other schools he fancied, including his dream school. To be fair, between an athletic scholarship and financial aid, the coach did secure most of the funding of the player's tuition and expenses. But in the end, the coach's college was the only one that the player visited or officially pursued. And that's the school at which he wound up. The player's lack of sophistication allowed the coach to figuratively wrap the player in his arms and keep him from considering other schools. Other than the majority of tuition thing, that is not a scenario most parents would want for their child.

A scenario like this is the furthest thing from your mind when you enter the club soccer world at U10-

11, and the presence of college coaches within the club can seem like (and often is) a very positive thing, but be aware of this possible trap for the unwary.

Win the College Recruiting Game

-14-

The Vagaries of the Recruiting Journey

I have hopefully made clear that the recruiting process is often an unpredictable one, with some twists and turns along the way. Despite the best laid plans, despite a case of a youth club and its coaches doing the right thing and affirmatively trying to help in the process, things can go awry.

In earlier chapters I have detailed the hiccups which occurred in the recruiting experiences of both of my sons, despite how involved I am in the sport, and how much I knew/thought I knew about the recruiting process.

But I also thought it might be useful to share with you one anecdote which shows how quickly things can change – positively or negatively – along the recruiting process.

My older son Noah had a goalkeeper teammate on the Boston Bolts Development Academy team, who at a certain point left for the MLS New England Revolution Development Academy team.[26] Things did not work out as hoped for with the Revs, so the young man moved once again – this time to a strong youth club which was not a U.S. Development Academy club.

I am good friends with the young man's dad, and he asked me to coffee to discuss a concern of his: namely, since his son was no longer in the DA, would he be deprived of good recruiting opportunities given that he would not be playing in the DA showcases (then played at Lakewood Ranch, FL in December, and Dallas, TX or Westfield, IN in June). We met for coffee, and at that initial meeting on the subject, the dad told me that his son was not being recruited by any college.

Noah had been receiving a lot of interest from many schools, so I had to be diplomatic, as I talked through the concern with the dad and reassured him. We met several times more in the ensuing months, and each time the story was similar – the man's son was not receiving any significant recruiting interest.

---

[26] There were at that time only two full Development Academy (now MLS Next) clubs in the greater Boston area – the standalone youth soccer club Boston Bolts, and the youth academy of the Major League Soccer team the New England Revolution.

The Vagaries of the Recruiting Journey

We later met again one workday morning in downtown Boston near our respective work offices, and I won't forget the occasion. The coffee took place at the Starbucks at the corner of Charles Street and Beacon Street near the Boston Common. I sat down with the dad, prepared to hear an update and to provide more advice.

But the dad had some significant news of the type that largely eliminated the need for my advice. Specifically, the dad explained that the son had recently played for his club team at the Disney Showcase in Orlando, and in one of the games he made an incredible save – a stretching fingertip save, which was attention-getting. It seems that when he walked off the field after that game, the Dartmouth recruiting coach approached him and made him a committed recruiting offer on the spot. Think of it! The young man had no recruiting interest going into the tournament and based on one strong game received an offer from one of the finest colleges in the country.

Hearing this news, I felt relief for the dad and happiness for him and his son. Yet, at the same time – and though there was complete mutual support and no competition going on between us – I realized that in some sense the tables had been flipped. Namely, despite all the interest in Noah that had come from college coaches, he had not yet received a formal D1 recruiting offer. It was around this time that I began to recognize that my reluctance to speak up about Noah being played out of position as a wing rather than center midfielder during his key recruiting years (as discussed in the Introduction and in Chapter 11), may have been a major mistake.

But this anecdote underscores the vagaries of recruiting. A previously unrecruited player makes one spectacular play at a showcase, and provided that the right coach (from a desired school) is present and watching, his/her entire recruiting experience can change 180 degrees to the positive. In contrast, if a player makes that great play or has a great game but that coach is either not present or is not watching at that moment, then the play goes into the ether, and is of no help to recruiting success. Further, if a player is high on a desired college's draft board, but the player happens to have a subpar game (every player has them) on the particular day that the recruiting coach comes to see them, the chances to be recruited by the dream school can be negatively affected and may even vanish.

The vagaries of the recruiting experience, indeed. The margins are that thin, and the timing that mercurial. The college recruiting journey is not for the faint of heart.

-15-

Avoid these Mistakes

As said in the Introduction to and elsewhere within this book, I have written this guide/book to pay it forward and to help you as a fellow parent – employing my personal knowledge and experiences to do so. In that sense, it would be somewhat incomplete and inauthentic if I did not admit mistakes I made along the way, meant as cautionary tales aimed at helping you avoid traps for the unwary along the college soccer recruiting journey. But in that sense, this will be the most personal and difficult of the words I share with you.

For the very most part, I am pleased and proud about the way I interacted with my two sons as their soccer coach, as a soccer dad within the club soccer years, and as a loving advisor in the college soccer recruiting process. There are, yet, several regrets I have and mistakes I made along the way – one in particular as a soccer dad, and four in particular within the recruiting process.

I taught both Noah and Josh the game from the earliest ages until and through intramural town play, and always kept it fun. I then coached both of their competitive teams in travel soccer. To honor the cardinal rule of coaching a team when one coaches their own child – namely, don't favor your child, in order to ensure that every team member gets treated equally – I sometimes bent over backwards to demonstrate the commitment to that value, and was a little tougher on them than on the other team members at times. For instance, there were occasions when I had Noah and Josh come off the bench in a game, even when their performance merited a starting position, just so it was clear to all that I was not favoring my own. I am gratified that both Noah and Josh have both told me that their travel team experiences remain amongst their happiest memories and days playing the sport.

And I am proud that despite Noah's early election of steadfast commitment to the U.S. Development Academy, I would check with him prior to every season to make sure that he was still happy in the DA, and with a gentle reminder of the possible opportunity cost related to not representing his high school. I know that being encouraging in the excruciating decision to leave the DA prior to his senior year when it became evident how unhappy Noah was – despite the admonishment that leaving the DA might reverse recruiting offers – was the right decision, because it was made out of love and for the emotional well-being of my son, despite any adverse recruiting consequences. Similarly, the solemn

Avoid these Mistakes

decision to have Josh leave the DA earlier on in the process when he was not getting playing time was made as a family, and with love.

But as I look back, here are the mistakes I made and regret:

The first relates to Noah's first fly away tournament in Virginia for his club team Boston Bolts when he was 12. On the first day of the tournament Noah's team had two games, and in the morning game Noah hid on the field, not showing for the ball, or running into position to receive it. Back in our hotel room following the game I told Noah that he had chosen to pursue club soccer, and along with a financial commitment for the family, that decision required greater playing commitment and dedication from him. In telling Noah that I recognized hiding on the field when I saw it, and that he owed it to himself and his teammates to be more present on the field, I raised my voice, and Noah understandably reacted emotionally.

In the second game that day Noah rebounded and played great, scoring the only goal in a 1-0 win. In the moment I thought that the serious conversation I had with him had helped him meet the moment, had taught him an important lesson about commitment, and had inspired him. But as I look back, I regret raising my voice to Noah (I believe it is the only time I ever did that within his playing career) that day, and wonder if he views it less as a teaching moment, and more of a negative, even slightly scarring memory.

The other four regrets I have concern mistakes I made within the recruiting process itself.

The first involves Noah's experience in the DA, and missing some signals of his growing unhappiness within it. As said immediately above and elsewhere in this book, I am proud that when it became clear that Noah had grown miserable in the DA – senior year after he had committed to a college – that love and caring for his well-being properly took precedence over the very real concern that his leaving the DA as a senior might take away an amazing college opportunity. Yet, as recounted in Chapter 8, Noah's answer prior to his junior year about it "not making sense" to leave the DA then, was in fact the first palpable signal from him that the DA was sapping his love and joy for the sport, and I flat out missed it. In hindsight, I wish that I had read into Noah's answer more thoroughly, and that a deeper conversation with him about whether staying in the DA was the right thing for him had taken place at that time.

I have already discussed the second regret at length in the Introduction and Chapter 11: namely, waiting too long to speak up (and the reasons therefor) when Noah was played out of position for a lengthy period during his key recruiting years. Thus, I won't rehash it in this chapter. I would urge you to read those sections of the book, and to heed the lessons set forth therein – namely, when you should be/should not be concerned when your child is played out of position (and correspondingly, when it is/is not appropriate to raise the matter with Club officials).

Avoid these Mistakes

The third regret involves the heavy early recruitment Noah experienced. In particular, Noah received his first direct email contact from the head coach of a top NESCAC school in 8th grade. I was first flummoxed, and then angry when I found out about a week following that email that Noah had not yet responded to the coach – in my mind, had "blown it off."

I scolded Noah for not appreciating the special opportunities he was in line for, and for not being properly respectful of the coach. I told him that so as to ensure that he was responsible in responding to coaches who wrote to him, I now wanted access to that email address so I could monitor it. Being responsible and respectful are two important values my wife Lori and I instilled in our boys, and it seemed most disappointing to see Noah's apparent nonchalance in this case.

In hindsight, I should have been much more understanding and looked much deeper regarding Noah's motivations. As time went on, it became clear that far from being spoiled or disrespectful, Noah was very much aware of the significance of that first recruiting email, and in fact was unnerved by it. To wit, he was only 14 and overwhelmed by having to think about college at such a young age. After all, the rest of his friends were still fully enjoying their youth, and were not in any way yet focused on something of the magnitude of college. In contrast, why should he have to think about and face the pressure of such serious life altering decisions at such a young age? I should have had a much more thorough and tender conversation with him at the time, to try to get to the bottom of his seeming misbehavior. I get it now and wish I did then.

This was the first time – and regrettably not the last – that Noah and I clashed around and within the recruiting process.

The fourth big mistake I made concerned summer ID Camps. As experienced as I am in the sport, Noah's recruiting was my first modern day personal recruiting experience, and I fell victim to a deluge of marketing emails, and some attenuated advice – which made me wrongly conclude that on the boys side a player should begin a regimen of ID Camps as soon as he is eligible – namely, the summer after 8th grade/of rising 9th grade.[27] In hindsight, I devised that approach out of comparative ignorance, and as I write in Chapter 5, in general (with limited exceptions) I recommend that on the boys side players don't begin participating in ID Camps until rising 10th grade summer.

Noah began the ID Camp odyssey in the summer following 8th grade. Given what I know now, that was clearly too early, for two main reasons. First, college coaches on the men's side – looking for their next recruiting class – are not going to focus on or give too much attention to someone who is merely a rising 9th grader. Second – and it frankly should have been a concern I recognized on my own – at that age, Noah was 3-4 years younger than most of the boys against whom he was competing, who were naturally much stronger and more physically developed than him. He called home the first night of his first camp (Yale/Wesleyan camp) demoralized that he could not keep up physically. When he yet found his rhythm

---

[27] The optimum time(s) to begin ID Camps -- different on the boys' and girls' side – are discussed in Chapter 5.

Avoid these Mistakes

and was able to perform well at each ID Camp that summer, I thought that it had become a non-issue, but in fact damage had been done.

The premature launching of an ID Camp "tour" that summer burned Noah out and made the experience a distasteful one for him. His 8th grade summer experience was so bad, such that he approached the following necessary/appropriate ID Camp years with dread and resistance, and it did not help in the recruiting experience. That was my fault, and if I could do it over again, I would have approached it and advised Noah differently.

Win the College Recruiting Game

Appendix: Insights from College Coaches

As you navigate this recruiting journey, I thought it would be useful for you to hear feedback on many of the points contained in this book directly from the college coaches themselves. I thus handpicked a list of college coaches whom I know and provided them with a Questionnaire to answer. I told them that they could answer as many or as few of the questions they chose (that's why some coaches answered more questions than some others). What follows are those answers verbatim from coaches from seven different colleges. (Note that the disparity in men's programs to women's programs relates to the yield of responding coaches who elected to participate.):

Win the College Recruiting Game

Insights from College Coaches

Interview 1: Head Coach · Division 1 · Men's Northeast Conference

What is your recruiting approach/philosophy?

We look for student-athletes who will be the right fit for our program and our university. We place a high premium on those who commit to being the best student, best athlete, and best person that they can be every day. We also place a high value on team players and those that understand that winning is a long-term process and a by-product of doing things the right way on a daily basis.

How many official recruits per year does the program normally receive from admissions?

There is no set number that we receive from admissions. We have an ideal roster of 30-32 and we can add them on a yearly basis as long as they are admissible.

Are there certain types of student athletes on whom you focus from a talent perspective (and conversely are there certain types of student athletes on whom you DON'T focus from a talent perspective – in this case, because you may not expect to get them)?

We focus on those who we feel can be successful in our environment. That would include student-athletes who are competitive, ambitious, humble, high energy, and tough enough mentally to deal with adversity. To be specific, we certainly look to play in a certain way, so we need players who are comfortable on the ball, able to play at increasingly higher levels for speed of play and defending as a group when we are not in possession.

Are there certain types of student athletes on whom you focus from an academic perspective (and conversely are there certain student athletes on whom you DON'T focus from an academic perspective – in this case, because you may not expect to get them or because you doubt they will be able to gain admission to your university)?

We are a very good school academically and the expectations for our players to achieve in the classroom are high when your team GPA is 3.50. So, it is imperative that we bring in people who are serious about their academic programs. For sure, there is a focus on those who have done well in their academic careers that is indicated by effort.

Which showcases/tournaments does your program attend? What are the factors which determine those choices (e.g., budget, quality, location, etc.)?

We attend games and events where players we might be interested in are playing. It is always a better assessment when the game is competitive against high level competition. Events where multiple players are competing make more sense for the budget. Specific events would be MLS Next tournaments, games, and showcases. Some ECNL events. There are also international games and events that we attend on a select basis.

Which ID camps does the program attend? What are the factors which determine those choices (e.g., budget, quality, location, financial interest, etc.)?

The only ID Camp we attend is our own.

How soon do you seriously begin to look at ID camp attendees (i.e., rising 9th grade summer, rising 10th grade summer, etc.)?

Realistically, we are always recruiting and looking for prospective student-athletes. It is probably heading into the 11th grade that things get more serious.

Does the program scout (in person) at high school games? If so, can you clarify whether they are private and/or public high school games?

It is rare that we would attend a high school game because it is difficult to get a proper assessment. There are times when it makes sense, and it does not matter whether it is a public or private school game.

To the extent that you do scout high school games, do your recruiting coaches scout club or high school games during the fall (when you are in season)? If so, with what frequency?

It is difficult to get out to games for recruiting purposes during our Fall season, but there are times when it is necessary. It depends so much on the level of the game and how it fits into our own schedule.

Does the program scout (in person) at club games? If so, teams in which league (e.g., MLS Next, the ECNL, the GA, the NPL, the EDP, etc.)?

We would scout games at any of the leagues mentioned. Once again, we would not cut off any opportunity when there is a player who may fit into our program and plans.

How many email contacts from players hoping to be recruited in a typical day/week do you receive (feel free to segment by time of year)?

We receive approximately 20 email contacts per day. We even receive that amount during holiday periods.

How long do you generally recommend a player's recruiting video should be?

Highlights about 5-7 minutes, but then a full game against the very best opponent you have played regardless of the score.

As a rule of thumb, does the recommended length differ depending upon whether the player is a) an offensive player; b) a defensive player; or c) a goalkeeper?

Insights from College Coaches

It does not make a difference of the position. For a goalkeeper, a training session can be included.

What is your in-state vs. out of state player ratio?

12:18

Win the College Recruiting Game

Interview 2 · Head Coach · Division 3 · Men's NESCAC Conference (New England Small College Athletic Conference)

What is your recruiting approach/philosophy?

Our overall recruiting philosophy is to bring in good players who are good people and keep them healthy and happy. We have built a terrific culture, and the older that I get, the more I want to be surrounded by positive people who bring good energy.

How many official recruits per year does the program normally receive from admissions?

There are so many moving parts as it relates to putting together a class in collaboration with admissions. For us, it's more about roster spots, and how you might fit the puzzle pieces together. Academic excellence, educational opportunities to succeed, diversity, etc. – are all ways that our school values applicants.

Are there certain types of student athletes on whom you focus from a talent perspective (and conversely are there certain types of student athletes on whom you DON'T focus from a talent

perspective – in this case, because you may not expect to get them)?

We try and recruit D1-talent players who want to receive a great education, to compete for a national championship and enjoy the balance that is so hard to attain in DI. It's a big pool, but I'd rather recruit one hundred DI players to get one, rather than take DIII players who are at the level.

Which ID camps does the program attend? What are the factors which determine those choices (e.g., budget, quality, location, financial interest, etc.)?

We only attend the Peak Performance Academy (PPA) camps because we run them on campus, and they have been such an effective recruiting tool for us. PPA is based around the idea that camps should be run by college coaches who are actually doing the coaching, and to help kids find the best fit for them – not by a business entity which exists to just make money.

Does the program scout (in person) at club games? If so, teams in which league (e.g., MLS Next, the ECNL, the GA, the NPL, the EDP, etc.)?

Yes, all of the above!

How many email contacts from players hoping to be recruited in a typical day/week do you receive (feel free to segment by time of year)?

Insights from College Coaches

I looked back and there were between 4,000-4,500 unique emails in our recruiting files for each year since 2015. These are people that reached out to us- so that's about 90 new kids every week who we hear from!

How long do you generally recommend a player's recruiting video should be?

Four to five minutes is perfect!

As a rule of thumb, does the recommended length differ depending upon whether the player is a) an offensive player; b) a defensive player; or c) a goalkeeper?

No.

What is your in-state vs. out of state player ratio?

Only 2 / 28 on our roster this coming year are from Massachusetts.

Win the College Recruiting Game

Interview 3: Former Recruiting Coach · Division 1 · Men's Ivy League and ACC (Atlantic Coast Conference)

What is your recruiting approach/philosophy?

Persistence is the key to good recruiting. You have to make the recruit feel like nobody wants him more than your school. I also developed a player profile which established the ideal physical, mental traits for particular positions. I also looked at the recruit's potential to develop over the next 4 years.

How many official recruits per year does the program normally receive from admissions?

Ivy League allows you 6 slots. ACC schools don't have a limit on how many players.

Are there certain types of student athletes on whom you focus from a talent perspective (and conversely are there certain types of student athletes on whom you DON'T focus from a talent perspective – in this case, because you may not expect to get them)?

I focused on a recruit's desire to work hard with and without the ball, especially when losing. I would not recruit a player who gave up and refused to help his team when losing. Attitude when faced with some adversity tells you everything you need to know about a recruit's character. I also looked at how they interacted with their teammates and coaches. That interaction will let me know if that recruit can fit into the culture of my program. Certain players are not recruitable due to their standing in the game. They may be a national team player and they usually go to the top ranked programs in the country that would help further their careers in the professional ranks and with the national team.

Are there certain types of student athletes on whom you focus from an academic perspective (and conversely are there certain student athletes on whom you DON'T focus from an academic perspective – in this case, because you may not expect to get them or because you doubt they will be able to gain admission to your university)?

Obviously the Ivy schools have very high standards when it comes to admittance, so we focused on recruits who would be able to handle the academic pressure. The ACC school where I coached also had high academic standards, so we had to bring in recruits that could handle the workload as well as the practice and travel rigors of being at an ACC school.

Which showcases/tournaments does your program attend? What are the factors which

determine those choices (e.g., budget, quality, location, etc.)?

MLS Next Winter Showcase
MLS Next Playoffs
Generation Adidas Cup
International Showcases
These are all based on budget size. The Ivy League school's budget was unlimited so that allowed us to travel to see a wide range of players.
At the ACC school the budget was very limited and was prohibitive when it came to the recruitment process.

Which ID camps does the program attend? What are the factors which determine those choices (e.g., budget, quality, location, financial interest, etc.)?

The Ivy League school hosted a lot of ID Camps so we invited our potential recruits to attend. We also attended ID Camps of local colleges in the area, and quality was the major factor. At the ACC school we would attend some ID Clinics in the area which was based on quality and the level of interest we had in the recruit.

How soon do you seriously begin to look at ID camp attendees (i.e., rising 9th grade summer, rising 10th grade summer, etc.)?

This would be determined by the level of the recruit. If he was a national team player we would obviously try to look at him earlier but usually we would be looking at rising 10th graders.

Does the program scout (in person) at high school games? If so, can you clarify whether they are private and/or public high school games?

At the Ivy League and ACC school we would attend some private high school games only.

To the extent that you do scout high school games, do your recruiting coaches scout club or high school games during the fall (when you are in season)? If so, with what frequency?

We would get to probably 1-2 private high school games a month. This was all based on the level of interest we had in the recruit.

Does the program scout (in person) at club games? If so, teams in which league (e.g., MLS Next, the ECNL, the GA, the NPL, the EDP, etc.)?

MLS Next, ECNL and NPL.

How many email contacts from players hoping to be recruited in a typical day/week do you receive (feel free to segment by time of year)?

At the Ivy League program we would receive 50-60 emails from potential recruits per day. They came pretty all year round. At the ACC school we would

Insights from College Coaches

get 30-50 per day and they were mainly in the Winter and Spring.

How long do you generally recommend a player's recruiting video should be?

3-4 minutes long.

As a rule of thumb, does the recommended length differ depending upon whether the player is a) an offensive player; b) a defensive player; or c) a goalkeeper?

The length does differ for Goalkeepers as you can see some strengths and weaknesses in practice. I encourage GK's to send longer videos.

What is your in-state vs. out of state player ratio?

Ivy League 1:5
ACC 2:5

Win the College Recruiting Game

Interview 4: Head Coach · Division 3 · Women's UAA Conference (University Athletic Association Conference)

What is your recruiting approach/philosophy?

My recruiting philosophy is to recruit not only talented players but to recruit good people. I try to prioritize building good relationships with recruits. I enjoy learning about their life outside of soccer, including school, family, and what they enjoy outside of sport. My goal is to develop these young players on and off the field, and my goal is to recruit players who want to grow and improve through respectful, constructive feedback.

Which showcases/tournaments does your program attend? What are the factors which determine those choices (e.g., budget, quality, location, etc.)?

We attend all ECNL showcases and GA showcases, and 2 DPL showcases, and all local showcases. We factor quality and budget. We fundraise to attend the cross country events and when we are at the local showcases we tend to recruit from the highest bracket. Being a division III program, we do try and find players from the DPL or other local events where players are standing out and making an impact for their team and in the game.

Which ID camps does the program attend? What are the factors which determine those choices (e.g., budget, quality, location, financial interest, etc.)?

Harvard, Brown, Yale, ID Sports USA, NE Top 100, MAP ID Clinic – we take into account, Budget, Quality, Academic similarities (ivy league schools).

How soon do you seriously begin to look at ID camp attendees (i.e., rising 9th grade summer, rising 10th grade summer, etc.)?

Rising 10th grade summer

Does the program scout (in person) at high school games? If so, can you clarify whether they are private and/or public high school games?

Yes, but typically players we have seen in the club setting and want to get an extra look at. This is pretty evenly divided between public and private.

To the extent that you do scout high school games, do your recruiting coaches scout club or high school games during the fall (when you are in season)? If so, with what frequency?

We don't scout club games in person during the fall.

Insights from College Coaches

Does the program scout (in person) at club games? If so, teams in which league (e.g., MLS Next, the ECNL, the GA, the NPL, the EDP, etc.)?

ECNL, the GA, the NPL, DPL, the EDP.

How many email contacts from players hoping to be recruited in a typical day/week do you receive (feel free to segment by time of year)?

Typical day – 5-10 recruit emails/day.

How long do you generally recommend a player's recruiting video should be?

3-5 minutes.

As a rule of thumb, does the recommended length differ depending upon whether the player is a) an offensive player; b) a defensive player; or c) a goalkeeper?

No

What is your in-state vs. out of state player ratio?

50/50

Win the College Recruiting Game

Interview 5: Head Coach · Division 1 · Men's Ivy League Conference

What is your recruiting approach/philosophy?

- *Identifying our positional needs*
- *Getting to know the player's personality*
- *Watching the player play in person as much as we can: warm ups, game, post-game to see all different interactions*
- *See how the player interacts with parents*
- *Do they fit the values of the program through their actions and through their conversations with our coaches, and our players?*

How many official recruits per year does the program normally receive from admissions?

Between 6-8.

Are there certain types of student athletes on whom you focus from a talent perspective (and conversely are there certain types of student athletes on whom you DON'T focus from a talent perspective – in this case, because you may not expect to get them)?

Yes, those players who maybe are not able to be coached or who are focused on things that we feel are outside of what truly matters are players we will look to stay away from.

Are there certain types of student athletes on whom you focus from an academic perspective

(and conversely are there certain student athletes on whom you DON'T focus from an academic perspective – in this case, because you may not expect to get them or because you doubt they will be able to gain admission to your university)?

Not particularly. We are fortunate that a lot of players will possibly want to attend the school for what it is. I prefer to find some of the players that might not have been able to attend and never saw themselves as being able to attend but soccer opened that door for them.

Which showcases/tournaments does your program attend? What are the factors which determine those choices (e.g., budget, quality, location, etc.)?

Attend MLS Next, ECNL, USYS, high school games and showcases, ID camps. We feel we do need to go where everyone is, but also want to go to the places where people might not be going to see players.

Which ID camps does the program attend? What are the factors which determine those choices (e.g., budget, quality, location, financial interest, etc.)?

Like to attend school specific camps and do work some non-school specific camps. Like to work the camps where there is a heart and soul to the camp, real instruction and teaching going on and not just a money maker.

Insights from College Coaches

How soon do you seriously begin to look at ID camp attendees (i.e., rising 9th grade summer, rising 10th grade summer, etc.)?

Between Sophomore and Junior Year is likely the best year.

Does the program scout (in person) at high school games? If so, can you clarify whether they are private and/or public high school games?

Yes and either school setting games.

To the extent that you do scout high school games, do your recruiting coaches scout club or high school games during the fall (when you are in season)? If so, with what frequency?

When training or game schedule permits.

Does the program scout (in person) at club games? If so, teams in which league (e.g., MLS Next, the ECNL, the GA, the NPL, the EDP, etc.)?

Yes, whenever possible in person, multiple times. Any of those mentioned leagues.

How many email contacts from players hoping to be recruited in a typical day/week do you receive (feel free to segment by time of year)?

Between 15-20.

How long do you generally recommend a player's recruiting video should be?

Depends on what the player is trying to convey about themselves and what our needs are for the position. That is hard for them to know because at the end of the day it is our determination about our need.

As a rule of thumb, does the recommended length differ depending upon whether the player is a) an offensive player; b) a defensive player; or c) a goalkeeper?

Not particularly.

What is your in-state vs. out of state player ratio?

We have about 3-5 players from in state; out of 28.

Interview 6: Head Coach · Division 1 · Women's Ivy League Conference

What is your recruiting approach/philosophy?

We filter through soccer ability first, then try to simultaneously look at character traits and academics to see if the player is a good fit for the program. If we have a pool of quality players, we hope to find great people who are committed students. We've found it's much easier this way than looking at great students to see if they are great soccer players.

Are there certain types of student athletes on whom you focus from a talent perspective (and conversely are there certain types of student athletes on whom you DON'T focus from a talent perspective – in this case, because you may not expect to get them)?

We need to find a balance of traits, so we focus on players that we believe can impact our environment, but not necessarily right away and not always in the position they play in club. We try to identify what talent can become in our environment. Recruiting a ball winning central midfielder is going to look a lot different to recruiting a crafty winger.

Are there certain types of student athletes on whom you focus from an academic perspective (and conversely are there certain student

athletes on whom you DON'T focus from an academic perspective – in this case, because you may not expect to get them or because you doubt they will be able to gain admission to your university)?

We expect our recruits to be committed students that have a strong transcript which demonstrates that they have challenged themselves academically. Students that have not challenged themselves academically with their course selection are challenging cases to consider.

Which showcases/tournaments does your program attend? What are the factors which determine those choices (e.g., budget, quality, location, etc.)?

We attempt to recruit at the major events and showcases as well as local events and international competitions.

Which ID camps does the program attend? What are the factors which determine those choices (e.g., budget, quality, location, financial interest, etc.)?

We typically only attend our own clinics.

How soon do you seriously begin to look at ID camp attendees (i.e., rising 9th grade summer, rising 10th grade summer, etc.)?

There are some very talented players that attend clinics; we certainly take note of the younger attendees so we can track them. The 9th, 10th and

Insights from College Coaches

11th graders are all being evaluated for their respective player pools.

Does the program scout (in person) at high school games? If so, can you clarify whether they are private and/or public high school games?

No, but we may go to a high school game of a recruit who we are familiar with.

To the extent that you do scout high school games, do your recruiting coaches scout club or high school games during the fall (when you are in season)? If so, with what frequency?

Very little recruiting during the fall. We host recruits on campus and continue to build relationships.

Does the program scout (in person) at club games? If so, teams in which league (e.g., MLS Next, the ECNL, the GA, the NPL, the EDP, etc.)?

ECNL, GA, major tournaments.

How many email contacts from players hoping to be recruited in a typical day/week do you receive (feel free to segment by time of year)?

Fluctuates, but it's a lot. Around tournaments we may receive 300+ in a week.

How long do you generally recommend a player's recruiting video should be?

3-5 mins, with an optional link to a half of a game or a full game if the coach wishes to see more.

As a rule of thumb, does the recommended length differ depending upon whether the player is a) an offensive player; b) a defensive player; or c) a goalkeeper?

No, but put the best clips first. It's good to organize into clip categories, but always lead with the good clips. Coaches may not give the video long if they are busy, so you want to catch their attention.

Interview 7: Head Coach · Division 1 · Men's Big Ten Conference

What is your recruiting approach/philosophy?

Assess team positional needs, then identify the players that have the highest caliber talent to fit that positional need. Evaluate the player's character qualities and academic profile to determine if they have the potential to succeed in our environment.

How many official recruits per year does the program normally receive from admissions?

7-8.

Are there certain types of student athletes on whom you focus from a talent perspective (and conversely are there certain types of student athletes on whom you DON'T focus from a talent perspective – in this case, because you may not expect to get them)?

Yes, we focus on the most consistent highly talented players. Reliability is a key factor.

Are there certain types of student athletes on whom you focus from an academic perspective (and conversely are there certain student athletes on whom you DON'T focus from an academic perspective – in this case, because you

may not expect to get them or because you doubt they will be able to gain admission to your university)?

Yes, we focus on student athletes who demonstrate a high work ethic in the classroom, not just high scores.

Which showcases/tournaments does your program attend? What are the factors which determine those choices (e.g., budget, quality, location, etc.)?

MLS Next fest, Dallas Cup, Generation Adidas Cup, ECNL national showcase.
Factors: highest concentration of national talent that we would not view live week to week. Also, MLS Next/GA record and post every game online, which allows us to verify our evaluations.

Which ID camps does the program attend? What are the factors which determine those choices (e.g., budget, quality, location, financial interest, etc.)?

We do not attend ID camps, however, we host our own ID camps.

How soon do you seriously begin to look at ID camp attendees (i.e., rising 9th grade summer, rising 10th grade summer, etc.)?

We create a database starting in the 9th grade.

Insights from College Coaches

Does the program scout (in person) at high school games? If so, can you clarify whether they are private and/or public high school games?

We scout at the New England prep school high school games occasionally.

To the extent that you do scout high school games, do your recruiting coaches scout club or high school games during the fall (when you are in season)? If so, with what frequency?

1-2 occasions.

Does the program scout (in person) at club games? If so, teams in which league (e.g., MLS Next, the ECNL, the GA, the NPL, the EDP, etc.)?

Yes. MLS Next, ECNL, GA, NPL, EDP.

How many email contacts from players hoping to be recruited in a typical day/week do you receive (feel free to segment by time of year)?

150.

How long do you generally recommend a player's recruiting video should be?

2-3min.

As a rule of thumb, does the recommended length differ depending upon whether the player is a) an

offensive player; b) a defensive player; or c) a goalkeeper?

No.

What is your in-state vs. out of state player ratio?

Ideally, 1 IN to 3 OUT.

Epilogue

There you have it. I hope this practical advice, interspaced with personal anecdotes, helps you in your approach to, and along the journey of, your child's college soccer recruiting endeavor.

When I look back, it still somewhat surprises me that someone as experienced in the sport as me could not have better helped both of his sons avoid the hiccups (and associated letdown) experienced in their respective recruiting journeys. So, this is my effort to pay it forward, with the hope that it will provide you with the best chance to avoid those hiccups. Again, this book/guide contains much of the advice I provide parents and players who personally contact me for recruiting advice. I hope that this information is helpful to you and your child along the college soccer recruiting journey.

www.ingramcontent.com/pod-product-compliance
Lightning Source LLC
Chambersburg PA
CBHW072054110526
44590CB00018B/3166